W9-AMU-024

Encouraging Achievement

by
Carolyn Coil

Pieces of
Learning

Cover design by John Steele
Graphic Production by Pam Jensen

©1999 Pieces of Learning
1990 Market Road
Marion IL 62959
polmarion@midamer.net
www.piecesoflearning.com

CLC0229
ISBN 1-880505-45-2
Printing No. 5432
Printed in the U.S.A.

Dedication

This book is dedicated with lots of love to

my two new daughters-in-law

Kristi Coil and Reba Coil

It's wonderful to have young women in the family!

and to

Beverly Job and my graduate students in DeKalb County, Georgia,

who constantly inspire and encourage me

Acknowledgments

Special thanks to:

Chris Kern whose Golden Archetypes Simulation Game gave me some ideas for the

Blockbuster Movie Review Learning Center

Ginna Hobgood for her ideas for the Orbit Around the Sun simulation

Janie Cohen-Legge who helped design the Evaluate and Classify activities

Kim Weatherly who developed the primary version of the Reliability of Sources Guidelines

Teachers who attended my workshops in Wake County, North Carolina, and gave me

suggestions and feedback on the Reliability of Sources Guidelines

ENCOURAGING ACHIEVEMENT

Table of Contents

**"TEACHING
IS ONE OF THE FEW PROFESSIONS
THAT PERMITS LOVE."**

Poet Theodore Roethke

> Leo is having lots of problems at home. His parents went through a divorce two years ago and his dad often fails to make the child support payment. It seems to Leo that his mother is always unhappy. She has a job, but it isn't enough to make ends meet. Leo finds school quite difficult. His teachers say, *"Oh, Leo! Yes, I know him! He's a behavior problem."* Leo knows he should study, but he really doesn't feel like it in school or when he gets home from school either. He used to think he was smart enough to go to college someday and maybe get a scholarship, but he just doesn't care about that anymore.

I met Leo several years ago when I was doing research on underachievement. At that time, I interviewed hundreds of kids who had been identified to me in one way or another as underachievers. Of all those students, Leo particularly stuck in my mind and my heart. He has become somewhat of a prototype for me — a student who exemplifies many of the problems we associate with those who are not achieving in school.

At first meeting, Leo was a strange combination of a child who was both depressed and defiant, defeated and angry, discouraged and daring. In our first interview, Leo would not look me in the face. He hung his head and shrugged his shoulders instead of answering my questions about his life and his schoolwork. I had evidence from early test scores that Leo was quite intelligent, but I would not have known that from his behavior.

Later, when his answers showed his anger and defiance, I realized that Leo was acting out his frustrations in the only way he knew how and toward the only environment in which he felt he had any control. School meant some form of stability for Leo, someplace where he knew the boundaries and rules and found it safe to rebel against them. Every other part of his environment was so insecure there was no way to rebel or to control it. So the school and his teachers received the consequences of the life he lived outside of the school day.

Leo is like thousands of other children who are at risk of failing - of not succeeding in school and of leaving school before they have adequate education and skills to meet the demands and challenges of the 21st century. They are often more concerned about problems at home than they are about doing well in school. They play the role of rebel or troublemaker because that role is a comfortable one. To succeed, these students need the stability and boundaries school can provide and they need encouragement from the significant adults in their lives.

Other types of students need our encouragement as well:

- High ability and gifted students who claim to be **bored** in school because they are not being challenged
- Teenagers who think it looks cool when they don't study
- The class clown who gets his identity from his jokes
- Struggling students who find learning difficult
- Adolescent females who don't want to look smarter than the males

You could add other categories to this list, for there are so many different needs and so many groups of students who need encouragement!

As educators we face the daunting task of encouraging students to achieve and do their best even when they have no desire to do so. As challenging as it might be, this effort is very worthwhile! There is a growing body of evidence that school failure is not inevitable. Our encouragement can produce lasting effects in improving the school achievement of these students.

As I began thinking about this book, the word **encourage** came to me over and over again. It seemed to me that this is what all of us try to do both with our students and with our own children. We try to cheer them on and hope they have the inner strength and courage to always do their best.

I looked up the word **encourage** in the thesaurus and was amazed to find over 100 words listed. As I read the list, I began to have a broader view of what is possible when we become encouragers.

Read a sampling of the synonyms for **encourage** on the next page. As you read each word, jot down the first thing that comes to your mind in relation to a student or students. Then share your thoughts with a colleague and discuss how each of you could take on the role of an encourager with your students or your own children.

The purpose of this book is to help you encourage achievement. Each chapter has numerous practical strategies and ideas that are easy to implement and use. As you read, choose the ones that best suit your teaching style, schedule, personality and situation. It is my hope that through this book I will be an encourager for you!

TEACHER REFLECTION PAGE
ENElhasURAGE - WHAT DOES IT MEAN?

Directions: Below are 19 words identified in the thesaurus as being synonyms of 'encourage.' Think about your students and write what comes into your mind as you consider each of the words below. Then discuss your thoughts with a colleague or small group.

1. advocate

2. aid

3. assist

4. bolster

5. cultivate

6. develop

7. exhort

8. foster

9. goad

10. grow

11. inspire

12. instigate

13. lead on

14. nurture

15. promote

16. propel

17. stimulate

18. strengthen

19. urge

Reproducible

TRAITS
AND
CHARACTERISTICS
OF STUDENTS WHO NEED SPECIAL ENCOURAGEMENT

> *"I can't wait!"* five-year-old Manuel confided to his older sister. *"Just four days to go until my very first day of school."* He jumped up and down with excitement. She looked at him in amazement. *"Why are you so excited about going to that place?"* she asked, as her shoulders slumped in apprehension.

Most children enter school full of high expectations and enthusiasm. By the end of first or second grade, however, many become discouraged and decide that they are not going to succeed in school. Instead of seeing learning as fun and challenging, they begin to see it as punishing, demeaning or boring.

How does this happen? What occurs within the first year or two of school that sets up some children for a life of school failure? What can we as teachers, administrators and parents do to encourage these students? These questions have multiple and complex answers. There is no one cause of underachievement and no one strategy for encouraging achievement in school. In this book we will look at many different approaches and strategies.

However, our first task must be to understand the many factors that contribute to underachievement and discouragement with school and all that is associated with it. There are numerous causes for this immense problem. In this chapter we will look at sev-

eral traits typical of students who need special encouragement to achieve. In subsequent chapters we will examine the role of the school, the role of the family, the role of society and a variety of other factors. In each chapter are various strategies for the specific topic.

Sometimes in workshops teachers ask me for the **magic formula** or the **silver bullet** which will reverse underachievement. Unfortunately there is no such thing! The best we can do is remember that working with children is an art, not a science. In that vein, let us begin to explore ways to encourage achievement.

Characteristics of Students who Need Encouragement

1. Unmotivated to do schoolwork

When I began my work about underachievers several years ago, my main premise was that I needed to find a way to motivate these students. To my surprise, I found that many underachievers are quite motivated, but they are not motivated to do **schoolwork**. I quickly learned that they are often intrinsically motivated, but this motivation is very dependent upon what the activity or task is. Underachieving students do not usually sit quietly and do nothing. They engage in a variety of activities that disturb or entertain their classmates, upset the teacher, and sabotage their own learning. They need encouragement to achieve **in school**!

2. Behavior problems

Poor behavior seems to be a defining characteristic of many students who do not succeed in school. Sometimes this behavior is quite humorous (except to the teacher) and other times it reflects hostility and violence. Students who misbehave not only disrupt other children, they also disrupt their own learning. It is almost impossible to be involved in learning when one spends much of his or her time in class engaged in unproductive and negative behaviors!

NOTES

3. Social immaturity

Often the students most at-risk for school failure are those who seem very immature when compared to their same age peers. They cannot sit quietly and listen to the teacher, they may have poorly developed small muscle skills, and they are just generally less mature than the other children. Often their chronological age does not match their maturity level, yet because of age driven compulsory education laws, all students enter school whatever their maturity levels.

4. Low self-esteem and low self-confidence

Self-esteem is your **perception** of what others think about you. These perceptions are the result of information that comes from the **outside** to the **inside**. When students feel they lack the love and approval of parents, other family members, teachers, other significant adults and their peers, their self-esteem is very low. Many students who need encouragement to achieve grow up feeling unloved and rejected and, as a result, they have extremely low self-esteem.

Self-confidence is the opposite side of the coin from self-esteem. It comes from the **inside** and goes to the **outside**. Self-confidence occurs when children realize they can control the **outcomes** of their lives and that personal actions and decisions make a difference in what happens to them. Students who need encouragement to achieve often feel they have absolutely no control over the events occurring in their lives. Consequently, they usually possess very little self-confidence.

Your students' beliefs and their attitudes about themselves are important considerations when we examine their self-confidence and self-

esteem. Think about the levels of achievement you could predict by listening to these four students:

> *"I have the ability to learn this subject or do this assignment."*
> *"I know I can succeed in this class with this teacher."*
> *"I'm just stupid anyway, so why try?"*
> *"That teacher hates me, so even if I study I won't do well on the test."*

The last two quotations reflect **learned helplessness.** These children feel they have no control over their lives. This attitude may result from an experience with an important uncontrollable event. It may come from having such negative expectations about the future that the child decides not to try. Remarks from the teacher may reinforce it, such as *"You never even try,"* or *"You're a hopeless case!"*

5. Lack of academic skills necessary to complete assigned tasks

Many students who need special encouragement to achieve begin school with minimal academic skills and poor language proficiency. Most of these students fall further and further behind their classmates. Each year it becomes almost impossible for them to catch up and learn the needed academic skills. Some of these students simply give up. This can happen as early as second or third grade.

The problem is that such students lack basic skills. They don't know process skills in math such as tables or formulas and find it difficult to do the more advanced problem solving correctly even if they understand the concepts. They may cover up

NOTES

this problem by copying another student's answers, looking up the correct answer in the back of the book or not doing the work at all.

One reason for this problem is that children who move from school to school often miss basic skills along the way. For example, if they teach percentages in School A in January and in School B in March, a child who moves from School B to School A at the end of February would miss instruction in this skill.

Other students lack basic research skills. This leads to copying directly from the book and calling it **research**. See **"Independent Learning Activities"** for specific strategies to guide students in doing effective research.

We need to be concerned about the *Swiss cheese* child. This is the student who has many academic holes in his learning. Often he gets by on what he innately knows, but as the years go by develops more and more academic holes. Figuratively speaking, the learning abilities of these students look like a piece of Swiss cheese filled with holes!

NOTES

6. No organizational skills

A descriptor I often hear about underachievers is **disorganized.** Students who do poorly in school are often very disorganized. They have a hard time keeping track of everything - their assignments, schedules, books, papers, pencils, pens, jackets, etc. School success assumes a certain amount of organization by the student. Without these skills even a highly intelligent child is liable to do poorly in school.

7. Influenced by peers who are poor role models

The old saying *"Birds of a feather flock together"* is true of students who are not achieving in school. These students seem to find one another and learn from one another, but in negative ways. Their peers influence students, and it is disastrous when one student influences another in a negative way. A child who has always enjoyed a certain sport, for example, may decide not to participate due to peer pressure. He or she may decide that looking smart isn't cool or refuse to carry books home to do homework at night. These students frequently end up not achieving and not working up to their ability levels.

8. Boredom with schoolwork

The mantra of many school-aged children seems to be, *"School is boring!"* Students with this attitude see no real life purpose for the learning they do in school. Ironically, they are often quite right. Many low achievers spend their days in school being taught a boring skills-based curriculum and doing endless skill-and-drill worksheets.

NOTES

One way to encourage achievement is to provide exciting, hands-on classroom activities and an integrated thematic approach to learning.

Another approach is to point out that much of life may **seem** boring, but people can enjoy even those things that seem boring. After all, books, paper and pencils probably seem boring to most children compared to TV, videos and computer games. If a child asks, *"Do I have to?"* when given an assignment, your response might be, *"No you get to. What a privilege learning is!"*

9. Rebellion against authority

Adolescents, particularly males, seem prone to rebellious attitudes and activities. From their point of view the **system** has not served them well and this translates into rebellion against the authority figures at hand, usually parents, school authorities and the police. These beliefs about themselves and their relationships to authority figures often translate into a lack of interest in achieving at school.

Two Beginning Strategies to Encourage Achievement

1. Recognize and work on academic holes and skill deficits.

- Identify academic holes through incidental observations and through more formal diagnostic tests.
- Don't assume the knowledge and skills are there. Even very bright students sometimes have academic holes.
- Do task analysis, giving the student step by step instructions on how best to complete the task.
- Develop a skills' profile or checklist for each student and pass it to the next teacher.
- Integrate the teaching of skills into relevant content areas. Allow students a choice in learning activities if they can learn the same skill in a variety of ways.
- Use learning centers for skills practice, enrichment and as a motivator.

2. Build self-confidence.

- Use dialog journals with focus questions to encourage student/teacher communication. These journals can boost self-confidence as a student and the teacher carry on a written dialog with one another.
- Help students see the connections between their actions and what happens in their lives.
- Use learners' logs for student reflections about the process of learning.
- Avoid encouraging or perpetuating self-pity or a student's attitude that says *"I can't."*
- Meet with individual students regularly to talk about how they are doing in school, about their friends or problems and anything else they want to discuss.

NOTES

NOTES

- Give students an opportunity to share something about themselves, their hopes and dreams with you.
- Take time to know your students and their lives outside school. Attend special activities outside class which involve your students.

These strategies are just the beginning. You will discover many more throughout this book.

Having once decided to achieve a certain task, put forth the necessary effort to achieve it well. The gain in self-confidence from such an accomplishment is immense.

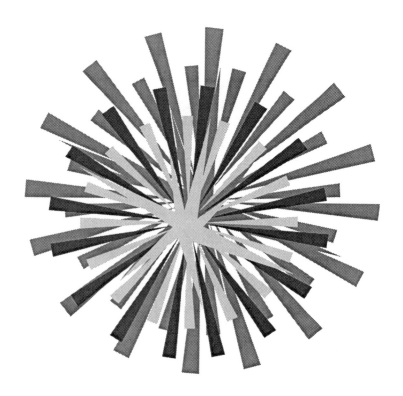

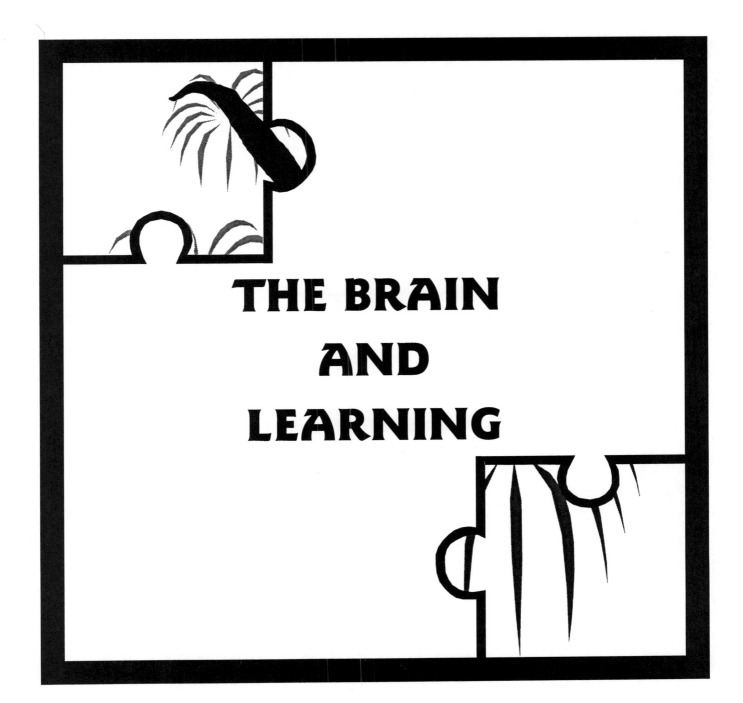

THE BRAIN AND LEARNING

"If I only had a brain!" laments the scarecrow in **The Wizard of Oz.** *"My head I'd be scratching while my thoughts were busy hatching . . . I'd unravel every riddle for any individual in trouble or in pain . . . if I only had a brain!"*

Yes, the scarecrow knew something of the value of a brain as do the teachers quoted below. Have you ever felt like saying these words to your students?

"If you would just close your mouth and put your brain in gear you might learn something," an exasperated teacher told an extremely talkative student.

"I can't just open up your heads and pour the knowledge into your brains! You have to pay attention and learn it so it will sink in," the seventh grade science teacher explained to her class. *"How much easier teaching would be if I could pour the knowledge into their brains directly,"* she thought to herself.

The Human Brain

Until very recently, the functioning of the human brain was a mystery. As the above quotations suggest, we have always known there is a connection between brain function, achievement, and learning, but we really didn't know very much about how this connection worked. Because our brains were hidden away, protected by our skulls, no one was able to study them while they were functioning inside live human beings.

Now all of that has changed. Brain imaging devices such as Magnetic Resonance Imaging (MRI), Positron Emission Tomography (PET) and Nuclear Magnetic Resonance Imagery (NMRI) allow us to peer through the skull and see the actual workings of the human brain at the cellular level. Through such imaging, neuroscientists can see the brain's neurons and synapses and how they work under different environmental and learning conditions. Their discoveries have exciting implications for all of us who want to know more about how best to encourage student achievement and learning.

The human brain is the most complex organism on earth. Although it weighs only about 3 pounds, it contains billions of cells called neurons. To give you an idea of the size of a neuron, you could fit 30,000 neurons onto the top of a pinhead! Neurons are wired together in complex ways through connections called synapses. The memory capacity of all the neurons in the brain has been compared to one thousand CD-ROMs, with each CD containing an entire encyclopedia set!

Babies are born with more than 100 billion brain cells, but these cells comprise an immature brain. Because of this immaturity of the brain, humans have long childhoods compared to other species. This means the learning that occurs in early childhood matters tremendously. In fact, a person's peak learning years come between the ages of four and 10, the years when the brain is developing and forming most of its synapses.

Learning occurs when the brain seeks connections to what it already knows. Because humans are social beings, much of this learning comes from interactions with one another. This process is messy and disorganized. Patterns, relationships, emotions and facts all fit together in some way, but they do not fit into a logical structure.

Furthermore, these connections in the brain form differently for each person, since each person's experiences are different. Thus, like individual fingerprints, each person's brain is unique in the way it is organized. No two brains are alike. Consequently, no one learning environment can completely satisfy two different people over an extended period of time. Our brains are individualized and our learning environments need to be this way, too.

According to recent research on the brain by Renate and Geoffrey Caine, every healthy human brain has the ability to:

- detect patterns
- make approximations
- have several different types of memory
- self-correct and learn from past experience
- engage in self-reflection
- analyze external data
- create in an infinite number of ways

Implications of Brain Research for Teachers

"We must take the time and effort to learn all we can about our brain and then figure out what to do about it."
Robert Sylwester, Emeritus Professor of Education, University of Oregon

This new knowledge about the brain has many implications for teaching, learning and student achievement. Many teaching techniques that encourage achievement fall into the category of what is now termed **brain-based learning**.

Brain-based learning implies that learning must be meaningful and must capitalize on experience. It relies on the fact that various subjects and disciplines relate to one another and share common information that the brain can recognize and organize. Because learners are constantly searching for patterns and connections on many levels, teachers need to help students find these and simultaneously make learning meaningful and personal.

The brain has **plasticity**, or the ability to grow and adapt in response to environmental stimuli. At birth the brain is genetically prepared to learn almost anything. It then uses emotion, experience, and previous learning to strengthen the useful connections and prunes away those connections which are unused or inefficient.

This concept of the brain's plasticity and the understanding that brain activities are linked by networks of neurons that perform many operations at once suggest that education should broaden its scope. Teachers need to integrate the entire school experience when planning curriculum. Unfortunately we often do just the opposite! When we want students to understand something, we usually break large concepts into smaller and smaller pieces.

We must do more than provide information and expect that our students will memorize irrelevant facts. Even when students accomplish this, they will never retain or translate it to other contexts unless the information has some meaning. So many good students cram facts into their heads and learn them for the test, only to forget them and never apply this learning at another time.

Brain research suggests that to encourage and enhance student learning, we must orchestrate multiple complex experiences within the curriculum. Instructional experiences which are challenging, interesting and require active thinking and student involvement are best. The brain will consider the entire experience and search for meaningful patterns. This suggests a need to teach our students via interdisciplinary, integrated, thematic instruction using many different resources.

Since students learn from **all** of their experiences, not just those that take place in school, real learning happens when they can see the connections between the things they have observed and experienced in all parts of their lives. Defining the direction of study with the students is important. Then allow them to go into depth on each subject, making connections to their own life experiences. When this happens students are challenged, are more creative and are better able to use higher level thinking skills.

When children think critically they must feel that taking risks is safe because they are likely to experience failure and make some mistakes along the way. Unfortunately, this does not usually happen in the traditional educational environment. In fact, with so much emphasis on high stakes standardized testing, schools are becoming places where experiencing failure is very stressful. Yet high stress learning environments do not encourage achievement! Instead, they produce emotions which are counterproductive to learning. We are discovering that emotion and brain function are interrelated and both affect student achievement.

Emotion and Brain Function

One aspect of recent brain research is helping us unlock the mysteries of how and where the brain processes emotions and how emotions affect attention, thinking and learning.

Emotion grows out of the limbic system of the brain. In the human brain, the limbic system and the neocortex (where the intellect resides) are interconnected, but emotions often drive action before the intellect gets a chance to intervene. Humans need this emotional response, for if we analyzed every action before we did something, we would never do anything at all.

Emotional responses from the brain have continuous implications in the classroom. Teachers have always known this on an intuitive level. How often have we planned to teach our students something but know it is no use until they resolve an emotional issue?

Emotion and attention are interrelated. Our brain culls out of the environment those things which are either dangerous or helpful to us. We use our emotions to decide what is important to learn and remember. Emotion drives attention and attention drives learning and memory. We know from our own observations that all kids learn more readily when they are emotionally involved. Concurrently, they are not going to learn anything if they're not paying attention to it or don't think it is important.

Paying attention is the key to the whole learning and memory process. For survival, our

brains have learned to size things up quickly and act upon that information. On the other hand, the human brain is not innately as good at things which require sustained attention and precision. This creates problems in school.

To thrive, the brain needs lots of stimulation. Conversely, it also needs **down time** to process what it has learned. Because of this, effective learning depends on emotional energy. We all learn things better when our emotions are engaged in the learning process. When we challenge our students to think critically and creatively, they generate emotional energy. They generate the same energy in a negative way when conflicts and behavior problems occur in the classroom or when they come in angry or upset about something that has happened at home.

There is the opposite effect to be concerned about as well. The brain considers too much stimulation as a threat. When this happens, it just turns off. Child abuse, poverty, malnourishment, and exposure to violence threaten many children's learning. This may result in a **downshifted** brain which experiences a sense of helplessness, fatigue, fear or anxiety instead of the excitement of a challenge.

The brain stores information based on functionality. In order for an individual to store information, the information has to have meaning and function for him. When traditional education seems meaningless, it can actually inhibit higher levels of learning. When students have no choice and teachers say, *"You must learn this,"* the excitement of learning may disappear. The brain downshifts and less motivated students no longer think critically, creatively or productively.

To encourage achievement, we must show students why the information they are to learn is or will be useful to them. This is quite a challenge for teachers! Thus, feelings, emotions and attitudes appear to affect learning. Daniel Goleman considered this when he introduced the concept of Emotional Intelligence during the 1990s. Three aspects of this intelligence are:

- *understanding one's own feelings*
- *empathy for the feelings of others*
- *regulating one's own emotions in a way that enhances living*

Emotional intelligence complements the types of intelligence measured by standardized IQ tests and is yet another aspect of intelligence to consider in addition to Gardner's multiple intelligences. The ability to handle stress and anxiety, for instance, affects a person's ability to analyze and synthesize something logically.

In fact, logical thinking and everyday observation tell us that emotions often rule people's minds. Emotional intelligence means having a sense of self-awareness or being smart about what we feel. When this awareness exists, the chance of handling it improves. Self-awareness is critically important because it allows our students to exercise self-control. Given sufficient self-awareness, people develop coping mechanisms.

Because emotions and brain function are so closely related, schools need to consider and work on this aspect of students lives. Children who learn ways to manage their anger, loneliness and frustration are then able to learn other things. Depressed or angry students literally cannot learn. Students who are involved emotionally in their learning listen more carefully, pay attention better, remember more and are better able to analyze and synthesize what they learn.

So often we educators put the cart before the horse. We want to encourage student achievement, but we begin with our learning outcomes and objectives rather than beginning with where the child is on an emotional level. Usually this approach is counterproductive and we then throw up our hands and declare, *"These kids just can't learn!"* Both brain research and common sense tell us to begin by helping students on an emotional level as they develop self-control and self-confidence before we deal with the academic learning outcomes of the day.

Most of the strategies suggested throughout this book are compatible with the findings of new brain research. Make sure you consider how the brain functions as you plan academic and affective activities for your students.

The Brain and Memory

A couple of years ago I visited a Maori village in Rotorua, New Zealand. The gate leading out of the village was an arch where (written in Maori) were these words: *"Hold fast to the memories, lest we forget."* Memories are very important to the Maori culture, and our guide had spoken about the value of cultural memory several times during our tour of the village.

As I reflected on that phrase, I began to realize that I had discounted the importance of memory and its significance for students who are entering the 21st century. In fact, I had often criticized memorization in schools, saying this was not a skill students needed in the Information Age. This walk through a traditional Maori village changed my thoughts, and I began to question my opinion of memory and its importance. During the last two years, I have come to believe that memory and the process of memorization are very important.

Memorization was once the forte of schoolteachers! They made sure their students memorized difficult words or phrases, whole paragraphs and stanzas. They assigned students to memorize poetry, drama, important historical slogans or mottoes, and political speeches. As a matter of course, all children memorized math facts, spelling words and geographical locations.

When was it that we began to discount the value of memorization? How did we forget that the joy of recollection through one's memory is a powerful motivator and encourager? Possibly this happened because the amount of available information on every conceivable topic has increased exponentially. There is no way we can memorize it all. Besides that, information on everything is just a click away via the computer! Learning something by heart, however, is different from clicking onto it on the Internet and printing it out. When something is learned by heart, it is with you forever.

Memory exists in many places in the brain. Perhaps this is why memorizing things is such good exercise for the brain. In much the same way that physical exercise is good for the body, mental exercise through memorization is good for the brain. Students who fill their minds only with **junk memories** such as popular songs, the words from television ads and sitcoms or phrases picked up in their peer group are feeding their brains **junk memories** exactly like someone who only eats at fast food restaurants feeds their body **junk food**.

We need to exercise our students' memories by giving them rich and important things to memorize! Poetry, phrases from classical literature, paragraphs from historical documents, famous sayings, quotes from Shakespeare and other writers - memorizing these types of things will encourage our students, enrich them culturally and at the same time exercise their brains!

Hold fast to the memories . . . lest we forget
Maori Proverb

Three Stages of Memory

Our memories have three distinct stages and functions. Each stage is important for its specific purpose. These stages are:

1. Paying attention to something and understanding it.

For anything to enter short-term memory, one has to give attention to it for at least a few minutes. When a person makes connections between the new information and knowledge one already has, we can say that they understand the new information. A hyperactive child or flustered adult may **forget** something because they weren't paying enough attention for it to go into the memory initially. Many of us hear things but do not really listen to what is being said. We see things but do not make the connections to understand what we are seeing. Such things will never even hit our short-term memories.

2. Sending the experience into long-term memory.

Once we understand something, the next stage is to remember it over the long-term. This happens through associations with other words or meanings, through visual imagery or via auxiliary elements such as smell or sound. Studying and reviewing information, skill building activities and direct teaching affects this stage of memory. Anxiety, stress, depression, joy, excitement, happiness and other emotions greatly influence this stage. Because of this, both encouraging and discouraging achievement may happen at this stage of the memory process.

3. Recalling the memory.

In stage three, a long-term memory is brought back from the unconscious to the conscious level. Someone who cannot immediately recall a specific item from his or her memory might say, *"The name's on the tip of my tongue."* Given time, and barring stressful circumstances, they can almost always recall the memory. Again, stress and other emotions may play a role and may block the memory. This happens to some students who cannot remember things they know during a stressful test but can recall it as soon as the test papers are collected!

Types of Memory

There are different types of memory. Each has different functions and is located in different parts of the brain.

Explicit and Implicit Memory

1. Explicit Memory - The system that stores concrete knowledge like faces, names and multiplication facts. This is the knowledge that a person calls up consciously. Most factual, knowledge-based tests deal with explicit memory.

2. Implicit Memory - These are memories not called up consciously but remembered automatically. Walking, serving a tennis ball or putting the brakes on in a car are all done through this type of memory. Someone with a brain injury may lose implicit memory and must learn these behaviors all over again.

Short-term and Long-term Memory

1. Short-term memory can hold from seven to ten items at a time. Short-term memory lasts only momentarily, and then the item is lost from the brain. We use this type of memory when we look up a phone number, copy a math problem or a spelling word from the board, or memorize something for the sole purpose of regurgitating it for a test.

2. Repetition causes items to go into long-term memory, probably into the cerebral cortex. This is where the brain forms individual connections, and over time long-term memory is what makes each of us individuals. No two people have exactly the same long-term memories stored in their brain.

We want our students to use all four types of memory during various learning tasks. When we assume that they have learned items in their short-term memories for the long term, we get in trouble. Often students cram for tests and exams and most of the information goes into their short-term memory. They then are unable to access or use the information later because it never entered their long-term memories.

A more productive way to increase student learning is to have students use what they have memorized in several different ways and with several types of experiences. This strengthens the connections throughout the brain and places what they have learned into long-term rather than into short-term memory.

Discourage **cramming for tests.** ***Encourage*** **learning and memorizing through a variety of experiences.**

Listening and Memory: Two skills that go hand in hand

Listening and memory are often interrelated. When you listen carefully, you are more likely to remember what has been said and to put the information into your long-term memory. The skills of listening and memorizing are important for students in the 21st century.

Why developing good listening and memorization skills is important for all students:

- Students who know how to listen and memorize tend to be higher achievers in school. Teaching all students the difference between hearing and listening is a first step in developing this skill. **Hearing** means having the words go from one's ears into the brain. **Listening** means having the words go into the brain and thinking about them once they're there! Many students hear without listening. Take time to practice the skill of listening with your students. For many this is a lost art. Being a good listener encourages achievement.

- The ability to listen to, process and commit new information to memory quickly so that it is available for recall is an essential 21st century job skill.

- The volume of available information <u>doubles</u> approximately every 14 months. A person who can listen and then incorporate this new information by connecting it to other information already in the brain's memory will be the one who will do well in the Information Age.

- Good listening skills help students in finding relationships between new information and the information they already know. Listening and understanding help the brain form connections and patterns.

- An effective memory and the ability to really listen increase adaptability and creativity. When connections are formed in the memory, new creative possibilities come to mind. Creative thinking is never done on a blank slate. It is done with the resources brought from the memories of past experiences and knowledge.

- Being a good listener and having a good memory are important social and intellectual resources. People who can remember the names of those they've met only once plus something about them are likely to be more successful socially and professionally.

Have a plan to teach listening and memorization skills. Integrate these skills throughout your curriculum and your school day. This is one of the easiest and most effective strategies for encouraging achievement.

Concepts about Memory

- Repetition helps memory. Thoughts wear <u>paths</u> in our memory. The more we recall the same information, and the more we put the same information into the memory, the easier it is for the brain to find it.

- Remembering things is easier when we <u>group thoughts</u> together. Pieces of information are easier to recall if they are associated with other similar information.

- Students need to <u>review quickly</u> after new information is presented. If they do not do this, 80% of all new information is lost within 24 hours. This is why it is easy to review and understand class notes the day after a lecture or seminar and why the same notes make no sense when reviewed a week or two later.

- Each person is the <u>director</u> of his or her own memory. Active listening is like being the director of a play or the coach of a football game. Each person decides what to pay attention to, which information to discard and which information is important to put into long-term memory. Good students can tell what is important and select this to incorporate into their long-term memories. (See suggestions in <u>Becoming an Achiever</u> by Carolyn Coil, Pieces of Learning, to help students know what is important to listen to.)

- <u>Visual images</u> often function as the icons of memory. As the old saying goes, **"A picture is worth a thousand words."** This is true with our memories. Like an icon on a computer, a visual reminder has behind it, stored in our memories, many verbal associations, events, facts and emotions. Test this idea by looking at an old photograph and using it as an icon for your memory. Then teach your students to use several different visual images as icons for their memories.

TEACHER REFLECTION PAGE
The Brain and Learning

✎ *With at least one other teacher, reflect upon and discuss the following questions.*

1. Brains are uniquely organized in each individual. How does that impact what we do as teachers?

2. How can we find the time to have our children involved in complex learning experiences when time in the school day is so fragmented?

3. How can we design the types of interactive, real-life learning experiences through which our students' brains learn best?

4. What memorization skills and techniques have you taught your students? From the subject or subjects you teach, what items do you think are worth memorizing so they will be in your students long-term memories for life?

5. Think back to a time when you were emotionally upset. How did this affect your ability to pay attention and to learn? Share this experience with a colleague.

6. How can we as teachers help students develop skills in emotional intelligence? How can we help them deal with the stresses and anxieties of their lives?

THE ROLE
OF THE SCHOOL

As educators, most of us do our best to encourage and motivate our students. However, we sometimes use phrases and have beliefs that result in just the opposite effect. Look at the statements below. How often have you said or thought something like one of these? Are there other **killer** phrases you use which may **discourage** your students instead of **encouraging** them? Having an awareness of the negative impact of your words or thoughts is a good first step in eliminating them!

Teachers' Killer Phrases that **discourage** achievement

I'll teach it straight from the book.

All the other teachers are doing it this way.

This is exactly how I learned it in school.

It takes too much time to change.

I'm counting the years until retirement.

I have to grade everyone in exactly the same way.

Don't smile until Christmas!

I have everything in my file cabinet to present my lessons.

I taught the same thing last year, so I'll use my old lesson plans.

I already made out my test so I can't change anything.

Of course, we do not want to discourage our students; in fact our goal is to encourage them! Educators and school systems as a whole can use many strategies to do this. The purpose of this chapter is to highlight some of strategies. We will look first at ways to encourage and meet the special needs of very young children. We will then consider the needs of all students.

Encouraging Achievement in Young Children

To encourage achievement, we should give children the essential services they require at their particular age or developmental stage. As teachers, we first deal with kids in preschool or kindergarten, during the early childhood years. When very young children begin school struggling, we want to do something right away! However, intensive early intervention for young children with no follow-up in improved curriculum and instruction in later years is unlikely to produce lasting gains. Mild interventions over extended periods may also fail to help low achievers succeed.

The good news is that intensive early intervention followed by improvements in ongoing curriculum and instruction can produce lasting results. Because of this, it is easy to understand that rather than allowing students to fail and then offer remediation, preventing school failure in the first place is far better. Trying to remediate failure later is more difficult because students who have failed in school are liable to be unmotivated, have poor self-concepts, and hate school. Failure in the early grades is almost a guarantee of failure later in the same child's school experiences. We must prevent the negative spiral that failure begins in some students' lives.

All students need to start their schooling with success, self-confidence, and a good foundation in reading. Teaching students to learn to read adequately during the first three years of school is by far the most important thing any teacher can do to encourage future school success.

On the next pages are several other strategies that focus on ways to encourage achievement in preschool and primary age students. If you work in early childhood education (with children or with their parents), these strategies will be particularly helpful to you.

NOTES

1. Encourage preschool attendance.

This helps students develop language proficiency, social skills and contributes to emotional growth. Attending some type of preschool program has a long-term positive impact on school dropout rates and school success.

2. Give struggling and immature students an extra year in the primary grades.

Identify children who are struggling academically or who lag behind their classmates socially and emotionally at the end of kindergarten. Give them an additional year to catch up before entering second grade. One way to do this is to assign those who appear developmentally immature to a developmental or transitional first grade which lasts two years. Another strategy is to identify these students and distribute them in each first grade class where they will stay for two years instead of one.

3. Form multi-grade classes where children can stay an additional year or complete three grades within a two-year period.

It is foolish for us to assume that all students will progress academically, socially and emotionally at the same rate. In a multi-grade classroom, students participate in a combination of homogeneous groups, heterogeneous groups, whole class instruction and individualized study. With flexible grouping, teachers can help students to progress at their own rate, compact the curriculum for high achievers, give remedial help to those who need it, and encourage all students as they develop appropriate social skills.

4. Offer a nongraded primary program.

Be flexible and regroup students according to skill levels across grade lines as they progress at their own rate through a hierarchy of skills. This is especially appropriate for instruction in reading and math.

5. Reduce class size in the primary grades.

A number of recent studies indicate that a reduction in class size in grades K-3 is one of the most effective strategies in boosting student achievement. Effective for the 1998-99 school year, the state of California implemented a new law mandating small class size in the primary grades. Other states are following suit. Reduced class size has the obvious benefits of allowing the teacher more time to work with each student, facilitating individualized and small group instruction, and targeting all students to develop proficiency in basic skills.

6. Use programs such as **Reading Recovery** which provide one-on-one tutoring.

These programs help prevent early reading failure, particularly for students in first grade, by targeting students who are having difficulty learning to read and working with them immediately. The longest lasting effects have been found in programs that use teachers rather than para-professionals or volunteers as tutors and in programs that provide one-on-one tutoring rather than small group instruction.

NOTES

NOTES

Strategies to Encourage Achievement in Students of All Ages

Think Positive!

> *"I really don't like school,"* complained Tywanna. *"The lunchroom is too crowded, my best friend isn't in my class, the teacher only calls on me when I don't know the answer, and all the boys are stupid!"* Her mother listened carefully and then said, *"I think you need to start looking for positive things to say about school."*

Many of us deal with students like Tywanna every day. While their academic work may be average, their attitudes are not. Negativity can do much to sap both enthusiasm and achievement. While teachers and parents cannot totally control a child's attitude, developing a positive classroom climate can help. Below are some strategies to help students think more positively about school and about life.

1. Start each day with a slogan for positive reinforcement.

You can find these slogans in books, on calendars, and even on signs you pass on your drive to school. In a culture filled with vulgarity, a positive slogan or motto will be a refreshing change. Write a new slogan on the board each morning to give your students a positive focus for the day. Some sample slogans are:

- All the beautiful things in the world are not as important as one kind action.
- Have a positive attitude. It's the first thing people notice about you.
- Invite the person behind you in line to go ahead of you.
- Life is 10% what happens to you and 90% how you react to it.

NOTES

2. Expose students to positive community role models.

Use motivational speakers to show students the possibilities for achievement in adult life. Local heroes are sometimes unknown and unsung, but they can be tremendous motivators and encouragers for kids. Start a list of positive role models in your area. Ask other teachers for suggestions. While many schools occasionally bring in a motivational speaker for the entire student body, someone who will come and talk just to your class or to a small group of students within your class will usually have more impact and a longer lasting effect.

3. Play music with positive messages. Encourage students to write positive lyrics to popular or well-known melodies.

In spite of the vast cultural wasteland of most pop music, songs that enlighten and inspire are still there. Look for new songs with positive messages and songs from the past that might appeal to your students. If your students enjoy certain popular songs but you don't like the lyrics, challenge them to write more positive and uplifting lyrics to go along with the music they like to hear. Music can have a powerful, positive impact on emotion, attitude and memory.

NOTES

4. Avoid comparisons with others.

Comparing one child to another rarely has a beneficial result. Feeling positive about oneself usually does not come from being compared to others. Even if a student feels he or she is better/smarter/more popular than others, a negative comparison is inevitable when a person falls short. Instead of comparisons, help students recognize their own strengths, talents, skills and abilities.

5. Have each student develop a self-pledge.

A pledge is a promise or commitment to do something. Many students know very little about pledges other than unthinkingly mumbling the Pledge of Allegiance each morning. Discuss the importance of making a pledge, particularly a pledge to oneself. Then ask each student to write a self-pledge. This can be done once each grading period and reviewed weekly or monthly.

A sample self-pledge and blank form are on the next page. Remember, this is a **self-pledge** which means it is something the child decides to do on his own. While teachers and parents can make suggestions or give examples, the pledge must be from the heart and a true pledge from the child. He or she should not write it to please the teacher or parents.

My Individual Pledge

Name _____ Terry _____

I pledge or promise myself that I will:

    * Finish my math homework every night.

    * Bring paper, pencil and pen to class every day.

I pledge or promise myself that I will <u>not</u>:

    * Give up when I don't get something right the first time.

    * Procrastinate until the last minute about doing a long-range project.

    * Ask to call my mom if I leave my homework at home.

I will remind myself of this pledge each day by:

    * Taping a copy of this in my locker and on the bathroom mirror.

My Individual Pledge

Name _____

I pledge or promise myself that I will:

I pledge or promise myself that I will <u>not</u>:

I will remind myself of this pledge each day by:

NOTES

School and School District Structure

The ways we plan and structure how schools operate can encourage or hinder achievement. Much of the school reform movement of the 1990s focused on improving student achievement through changing school structure. Innovations such as block scheduling, charter schools, wiring school computers for Internet access, site-based management and different school calendars and holidays are examples of this trend. Additionally, great emphasis has been placed on standardized testing as a way to improve achievement. Below are other strategies for encouraging achievement by changing the way we traditionally have structured schools.

1. Plan an April Fool's teaching event where all the teachers in the school teach someone else's class.

This works wonders by giving teachers a fresh perspective, new strategies, and possibly a greater appreciation of their own students. It is especially effective when teachers of primary students teach older students and vice versa.

2. Begin a Five-Year High School Plan for students who have academic weaknesses and need a slower pace and more time to master skills and complete course work.

This plan assumes that we are looking for competencies and skills rather than how many days or hours a student has attended a given class. We can say the same of the next strategy.

NOTES

3. Begin a Three-Year High School Plan for students who work at a fast pace and master skills and new information quickly.

Some students do not need a semester or a year to master the skills of a given course or class. Others may be able to attend class every other day and keep up with the work, making it feasible to sign up for two courses offered simultaneously. Being able to learn at a faster pace is a tremendous encourager for high ability students.

4. Begin a school for high school students who are night owls - not morning people.

Such a school could have classes beginning at 3:00 P.M. and going until 9:00 P.M. For some teenagers this is peak learning time! Sundown Night School in Thornton, Colorado, near Denver, uses this approach. They target students in a traditional school setting (going from 7:30 A.M. until 2:30 P.M.) who do poorly in morning classes but much better in their afternoon classes. They require these night school students to take a full load of tough academic classes and they generally do very well. Why do we have the idea that all students must learn best in the morning and early afternoon? Let's encourage achievement by changing the time some students attend school.

5. Explore the feasibility of Year Round Schools.

Many school districts have a few schools that are on a year round calendar. Often this is done to free needed classroom space, but there is an additional positive benefit to this type of scheduling. Students seem to retain more of their skills and

NOTES

knowledge base when they are in a year round program. When schools have a series of shorter breaks there is not as much time to forget the essential skills taught. Now that we are far from the agricultural economy which produced long summer vacations in the first place, the year round model is a good one to consider when a district is looking for ways to encourage student achievement.

6. Make sure the approach to schoolwork, assignments, behavior and homework is consistent between classes at the same school.

When everyone on the faculty holds the same expectations for students, achievement generally increases. This includes everything from how to head papers, take notes and organize assignments to what happens when a student is tardy or absent. A standardization program encourages achievement by eliminating confusion and providing a sense of consistency for students. Lester Middle School, a U. S. Department of Defense School in Okinawa, Japan, has had great success using this strategy.

7. Allow advanced students to accelerate to the next grade.

Contrary to popular opinion, research is almost uniformly positive about the results and effects of acceleration. Any school setting can use acceleration, and it is cost effective. Accelerated students do at least as well as other students in their classes, and because they are working at a higher level their encouragement to achieve is usually greater. Acceleration can include moving to a high-

NOTES

er grade level on a full time basis or for selected subject areas during part of the school day.

8. Use teachers as student advocates, mentors and counselors.

This type of program releases teachers from classroom duties 3-4 hours per week to meet with students and counsel with them on a one-to-one basis. While this type of activity is usually associated with the school guidance counselor, there are tremendous benefits when teachers also assume a guidance and counseling role. A one-on-one relationship with a teacher is one of the greatest encouragers a student can have.

9. Meet in grade level or departmental teams to brainstorm how to encourage and motivate specific students.

In the _Motivating Underachievers_ workshop, participants read brief written case studies of typical underachieving students. In groups, the workshop attendees brainstorm ways to motivate and encourage their case study student. It is always amazing how many wonderful, practical ideas come from this 15 minute exercise. If teachers would share case studies of their own students and brainstorm strategies for working with them, many good ideas would result in a very short time. This is a much more beneficial activity than complaining about students and how bad they are!

Encouraging Achievement: Is Testing the Answer?

"My class performed well on the state assessment tests, but when we got our scores back, I felt mixed emotions. I breathed a sigh of relief for the students, my school and myself. However, I also felt sad because this year I haven't felt the pure joy of teaching and learning together as much as years past. Our focus had to be on the test, and the joy of exploring the vast world of knowledge was partially forsaken. If we want children who can perform well on multiple choice tests, we have done well. However, if our intent is to form concerned citizens, motivated learners and creative problem solvers, I am not sure about our success."
— **Teacher, North Carolina**

America's growing preoccupation with testing is having negative effects in classrooms throughout our country. In most states, schools must report test scores, and in some places test scores can determine whether a school gets funding, whether a teacher gets merit pay or whether the principal will have a job the following year. In some states, school accreditation and high school graduation are linked to test scores.

Furthermore, the media often misconstrues and sensationalizes test results. The perception often is that a good school will have high test scores while a poor one will not. However, comparing the test scores involves so many factors that comparing the test scores of two schools is like comparing apples and oranges!

These higher and higher stakes attached to student test performance are forcing teachers to spend more and more time preparing students for tests. It is estimated that a full month of class time is spent in test preparation and administration. Test anxiety is high among students. Instead of encouraging student achievement, testing can create an emotional drain, especially if kids feel pressure to excel. First graders often cry, have nightmares and get stomachaches before test day.

According to Boston College's Center for the Study of Testing, American students take between three and nine high-stakes tests per year. These include state mandated assessments, tests for special education services, tests for college admissions, and a variety of other nationally standardized tests.

We can measure achievement in a variety of ways and a paper and pencil test is only one way. Supposedly standardized tests help ensure that students graduate from high school with the skills they need to succeed in the world. Students need to be creative and critical thinkers, problem solvers, decision makers and life long learners. However, the required tests may not be the best way to measure these attributes. While testing may focus teachers and students on competencies in basic skill areas, it is doubtful that requiring more and more tests is the most effective way to encourage achievement.

TEACHER REFLECTION PAGE
Testing and Achievement

1. Are tests diagnostic tools, tools for remediation or a way to hold teachers accountable? How are they used in your school district?

2. Teaching to the test has become an acceptable practice in many schools as has aligning the curriculum to meet testing standards and criteria. In what ways are these practices beneficial? In what ways are they harmful?

3. Should our goal be to encourage our students to be good test takers? If not, how should we measure student achievement and success?

4. A school principal in Chicago said, *"These kids could be drowned by tests . . . Don't test us to death."* What do you think she meant by this statement?

5. What are the benefits of testing in terms of encouraging student achievement? What would be your ideal plan for testing and assessing student achievement and progress?

NOTES

Individual Classroom Structure: Physical space

1. Be innovative about how you use your classroom space.

Adjust the physical arrangement of your classroom in any way that might encourage student learning. This includes knowing the best viewing distance for reading print materials, establishing locations that facilitate listening, and allowing students to decorate walls and bulletin boards with things that interest them. Use all classroom space for learning - don't overlook any unused corners or areas!

2. Make sure you can move quickly to all parts of the room.

Look over your classroom when no students are present. Are there any distractions to learning? Can you move quickly to all parts of the room? You can solve minor problems quickly if you can move to the location where problems are occurring. Scan the class frequently to notice and respond to potential problems or a minor argument. This response can usually be a mere verbal cue or walking over to the person causing the problem.

3. Change your classroom seating arrangement often.

Vary the seating arrangements in your classroom. Seat students so that they learn together but also so that they don't interfere with or bother one another thus detracting from learning. You can encourage achievement by flexibly grouping your students for some activities and allowing them to work individually for others. Change their seats depending on the learning activities in which they are engaged. Stand in different parts of the room when giving direct instruction. This makes it more **difficult** for students in certain locations to *not* pay attention!

4. Give students structured freedom to move about the classroom.

Classroom chaos does not encourage achievement! However, the freedom to move around while learning is helpful, particularly for kinesthetic learners. Set rules and procedures to structure movement. Then allow your students the freedom they need to move as they learn.

5. Display student work throughout your classroom, school and community.

As much as possible, your classroom, hallways and other locations within the school should be full of student work! Community buildings, shopping malls and other outside locations provide additional areas for display. Use these displays to provide learning opportunities for other students and to encourage your students to do even higher quality work on the next assignment or project.

NOTES

NOTES

Individual Classroom Structure: Classroom Organization and Management

> *"I think I'm doing most of the right things,"* first year teacher Ms. Durham thought to herself at the end of a particularly hectic day. *"But there are so many little details to remember and keep track of! How can I be positive with my students yet still maintain discipline? I'm not sure I know how to group kids and still be organized. I have lots of classroom rules yet the kids forget or ignore them. I didn't know there was so much to keep track of when you're a teacher!"*

Whether you're a first year teacher like Ms. Durham or a 30-year veteran, you know that classroom management and organization is one of the most important aspects of teaching. Each teacher develops his or her own management plan and style of organization. Explore some of the best strategies from successful teachers in the next few pages. Use and adapt them to best meet your needs.

1. Team each underachieving student with an achieving partner of *equal* ability to do a cooperative or collaborative learning project or assignment.

This gives the underachiever the beginning foundation for a relationship with a positive, achieving peer of approximately the same ability level. This is a much better strategy than grouping all of the underachievers together for remediation or punishment!

50

2. Have your students develop rules with you.

Display them clearly so they can see the expectations for classroom behavior in your classroom. Have few enough rules that every child in your room knows them all by memory! A long list of classroom rules serves no purpose if no one remembers what they are.

3. Plan ways to discuss specific problems in a positive manner.

Organize small advisor, counseling or conflict management groups to discuss current student issues. Provide time for class meetings to discuss student concerns and to deal with and solve minor problems. Be specific about what language is suitable in school if students' use of inappropriate language is a problem.

4. Greet each student by name as he or she enters the room.

Names are powerful! Just a simple greeting tells the student you acknowledge his/her presence and know that he or she is important.

5. Make sure students are responsible for cleaning up after themselves at the end of the class period or school day.

One thing that impressed me most when I visited schools in Japan was that the students were responsible for keeping their classrooms and their school clean. An everyday sight was students sweeping their classrooms with brooms and pol-

NOTES

NOTES

ishing desks and tables with cleaning cloths. Obviously we do not run our schools this way, but we can expect our students to keep their classrooms clean! This may take direction and encouragement from the teacher. Nevertheless, the effort is well worth it, not only because your classroom will be cleaner but also because this is a wonderful way to teach responsibility.

6. Monitor the noise level in your classroom.

Talking to your class when your room is noisy is difficult, if not impossible. Develop signals with your students so they will know when it is time to get quiet. One of my favorite techniques is to stand beside one group of students and say, *"If you can hear my voice, clap twice."* The clapping will get other students' attention, and then you can repeat the phrase. This technique will get everyone's attention in a short period of time without raising your voice! Whenever you notice your students getting a bit noisy when you are talking, decrease the volume of your voice as the noise level increases in the classroom. The noise level will usually decrease as well.

7. At the beginning of the school year, before any problems occur, contact the parents of each of your students just to get acquainted.

Like preventive medicine, this type of contact helps avoid future behavior problems. It is also a powerful encourager, because it sends the message that you care.

NOTES

8. When misbehavior occurs, immediately make contact with the student involved.

Do this with a glance, moving closer to the student, or asking the student for an on-task response. A calm and immediate response to a problem creates a positive ripple effect.

9. Avoid threats and appeals to your authority or the authority of those over you.

Kids today seem to live in an atmosphere of numerous threats but little action. A declaration such as, *"If you don't stop that misbehavior I'll send you to the principal"* has almost no impact on student behavior, and it can be a discourager for learning and achievement.

10. Have clear expectations about classroom behavior.

Set limits and expectations that encourage achievement and reinforce your classroom goals. Role play acceptable and unacceptable behaviors with your students. When students misbehave or become unfocused, remind them of the classroom rule or procedure they are not demonstrating. If necessary, take time for the entire class to practice the correct way to do something. Your clear instructions should include the following:

- What they will be doing
- Why they are doing it
- How they can get help if needed
- What to do with the completed work
- What to do when they finish
- What to do if they don't finish in the allotted time

Individual Classroom Structure: Transition Procedures

All students experience times of transition at several points during the school day. In elementary school, students go to special subjects, to lunch, to the computer room, or the teacher may simply switch to a new subject for study. Most middle school and high school students and even some elementary school students change classes several times each day. As this change occurs, students may enter the classroom excited, agitated or simply unfocused.

Transition times are the points during the school day when behavior problems are most likely to occur. If not used well, they may also be times when opportunities for learning are lost because transition time interrupts attention and concentration. Unless specifically guided, most students don't use transition times to review what they learned yesterday or get mentally prepared for the upcoming class or lesson. One way to encourage achievement in all students is to develop, guide and enforce good transition procedures.

Discuss transition problems (or potential problems) with your students and, with them, develop procedures and rules for making smooth transitions when coming into your classroom. These procedures should include a *warm up* activity each day. Brainstorm with your students what they might like as warm ups. A sample list is as follows:

- Journal writing
- Learning log
- Active questions
- Relaxation activity
- Listening to music selected by the teacher
- Listening to music selected by the students
- Brainstorming answers to the **Question of the Day**
- Sharing something already learned in school during the day

When doing your lesson plans, make sure you consider the transitions from one activity to another within your own classroom. Many teachers plan classroom activities well, but don't plan the transition times between the blocks. Look at your lesson plans. Even when you fill each block, you still have to consider the lines! These are your transition times. Some helpful hints for smooth transitions within your classroom include:

- Plan your physical classroom arrangement to facilitate transitions.
- Make sure the students understand the schedule or game plan.
- Have materials ready for what is coming next.
- Assign students some transition tasks.
- Have anchoring activities - on-going relevant tasks that students automatically move to when they finish classroom assignments.
- Design independent learning centers for students to work in during transition times.

Individual Classroom Structure: Curriculum and Instruction

NOTES

1. Look at individual instructional needs.

Plan lessons which give students choices and involve Gardner's Multiple Intelligences, a variety of learning styles and learning modalities, and all levels of Bloom's Taxonomy. Use various forms of assessment. Use checklists, journals, projects and performances to assess progress at least as often as pencil and paper tests. (See _Teaching Tools for the 21st Century_ by Carolyn Coil, Pieces of Learning.)

2. Provide high interest activities in which students are actively involved in learning.

Vary the learning activities in your classroom so that you meet all students' needs. Plan these activities around essential learning goals and outcomes. Try readers' theater, choral reading, chapter books, discussion groups, writing one's own scripts, video productions, and projects of all types.

3. Begin a lesson by getting the student's attention and including a motivator.

Plan an unusual cue or activity to get everyone's attention. Make sure distractions are at a minimum. This opening motivator may be the most important aspect of the lesson, for it may encourage attention and achievement throughout the remainder of the instructional time.

NOTES

4. Modify and adapt the materials and teaching techniques you are currently using in your classroom.

Making minor alterations may sometimes result in the possibilities of success for a student who needs lots of encouragement or who needs special help. As needed, provide outlines and other visual organizers which students can use to help direct their thinking.

5. Establish homework clubs and academic help sessions.

Students who need the most help with academics are the least likely to seek it, even if you are easily approachable and willing to give such help on an individual basis. These same students may be more open to participating in academic clubs, study groups or the like, especially if encouraged to do so by a popular friend or student. Enlist some of your well-liked students as participants in these sessions and have them recruit other students who could benefit most from extra academic help.

6. Help students plan, adjust and reflect on long range assignments by helping them break the large task into smaller segments.

Encourage students to complete long-term projects by helping them develop a projected work plan and how to reflect on their own work as it progresses. The sample **Record of Student Work** forms on pages 57-58 show how one student used this process. Us the blank form on page 59 with your students.

Record of Work for Product or Performance

Date	Work Planned	Work Actually Done	Adjustments to Plan for next day	Reflections on my work (Difficulties, strengths, surprises)
Monday	Find books and other information on the topic at home and at the library.			
Tuesday	Take notes from all sources. See what's on the Internet that I could use.			
Wednesday	Begin writing rough draft. Plan visuals to go with written report.			
Thursday	Finish rough draft. Ask someone to proofread. Work on visuals.			
Weekend	Do final report. Finish visuals. Put together in folder.			
Monday	Check to make sure everything is ready to be turned in tomorrow.			

Reproducible

Record of Work for Product or Performance

Date	Work Planned	Work Actually Done	Adjustments to Plan for next day	Reflections on my work (Difficulties, strengths, surprises)
Monday	Find books and other information on the topic at home and at the library.	Found one book at home. My mom couldn't take me to the library.	Now I need to go to the library tomorrow.	My mom was too busy and she is making me get behind. I wish I could drive.
Tuesday	Take notes from all sources. See what's on the Internet that I could use.	Went to the library and found a book and 2 news articles. Surfed the Internet but didn't see anything useful.	I need to work on the notes tomorrow.	I saw a lot of cool stuff on the Net but nothing that will help me with this report and project.
Wednesday	Begin writing rough draft. Plan visuals to go with written report.	Took notes from the books. Started making a collage.	I want to do the whole rough draft tomorrow.	My collage is good. It is turning out better than I thought. But I wish the rough draft was finished.
Thursday	Finish rough draft. Ask someone to proofread. Work on visuals.	Finished the collage.	Now I have to do the rough draft and the final report this weekend.	I hate homework on weekends. I leave the stuff I don't like to do until the last minute.
Weekend	Do final report. Finish visuals. Put together in folder.	Rough draft done. My dad proofread it. I got my folder and decorated it.	I have to do the whole final written report on Monday night.	I wish this assignment was done. My collage is the best!
Monday	Check to make sure everything is ready to be turned in tomorrow.	Written report finished. Everything is in a folder.	I am ready to turn this in.	I'm glad the teacher made us plan a "cushion day" in our projected work plan. That is the only reason this will be turned in on time.

Reproducible

Record of Work for Product or Performance

Date	Work Planned	Work Actually Done	Adjustments to Plan for next day	Reflections on my work (Difficulties, strengths, surprises)
Monday				
Tuesday				
Wednesday				
Thursday				
Weekend				
Monday				

"A teacher affects eternity;
he can never tell
where his influence stops."

Henry Adams,
The Education of Henry Adams

WORK, CHALLENGES, LEARNING & RESPONSIBILITIES

Work, Challenges, Learning from Failure, and Responsibility

Effort, Persistence and Challenges

School comes easy to 14-year-old Aaron. He never has to work or study to make good grades or to be on the honor roll. Everyone expects him to do well in school because he always has. He chooses easy classes and has no specific goals after high school. His teachers and parents consider him a good kid and have never thought about the fact that they should challenge him more in school.

Elaine is a quiet child. She never gets in trouble in school, but her teacher sometimes forgets she's even there. Elaine withdraws so no one will ask her a question she might not be able to answer. She hopes no one will notice her or call on her. When she can, she sits behind someone else so teachers won't notice her. Her goal is to get through school without making any waves while doing a minimum amount of work.

Students often retreat from challenge. *"This work is too hard,"* they might say, while their underlying message is, *"It should be fun; you should be entertaining me!"* Many kids whom we are raising in an era of constant entertainment through TV, video games and instant gratification feel that schoolwork has to be *fun* or they won't do it.

The problem is that learning isn't always fun or easy! Sometimes it is hard work. **The teacher's job is not to entertain students; it is to teach them**! The notion that everything should be entertaining has seeped deeply into American pop culture. TV, music, comedy routines, videos and computer programs all come with incredible visuals, sound effects and one-liners. Kids expect that learning should be that way, too. Like Aaron, they avoid the hard classes, choose the effortless assignments or projects, and look for the easy "A." Yet nothing can replace diligence and hard work in terms of achievement outcomes.

Kids often boast about not working. They avoid work, challenging classes and homework. Many do not achieve, particularly when a difficult assignment means they must really study or apply themselves. They may feel stressed out because the class is challenging and demanding, but they won't put forth the required effort. Instead, they become excellent procrastinators and think that somehow they will make it through. In the end, they do much less than they are capable of doing.

Encouraging Achievement by Praising Persistence and Effort

Many students react to peer pressure and try not to look too smart. They feel that the worst thing would be to seem like a nerd! Tackling an academic challenge and appreciating its rigor would be the last thing many kids would ever consider! How, then, can we encourage students to embrace academic challenges and choose the more demanding learning activities instead of always the easiest ones?

One answer can be found in a 1997 study conducted by psychologist Carol Dweck of Columbia University. She found that children praised for specific efforts or specific strategies they have used are likely to outperform classmates who are continually told they are doing well because they are intelligent and smart. When students hear the message that their work is good because they are so smart, they learn to measure intelligence only through their performance. Thus, when they make mistakes they falter. Somehow that shows they aren't intelligent anymore! On the other hand, students taught that effort is the key to success keep trying after failures and learn from their mistakes.

- *Students praised for their intelligence are more likely to view later failures as a sign of low ability and give up on trying to accomplish the task.*

- *Students praised for their intelligence are more likely to view their ability as unchangeable when faced with a difficult task.*

- *Students praised for effort try harder when faced with a mistake or failure.*

- *Students praised for being smart choose an easy task over a harder challenge.*

- *Students praised for effort choose harder, more challenging learning tasks.*

All of us, educators and parents alike, can learn a valuable lesson from this study. Praising children for being smart or intelligent is so easy! It is more difficult to remember to praise students for their efforts, even when they make mistakes, and for their persistence when they keep working on a challenging and difficult learning task.

Remember

Praise students for their persistence and effort rather than for their intelligence and/or how smart they are!

NOTES

Strategies for Encouraging Achievement in Unchallenged Students:

1. Do specific career or college counseling.

Ask, *"What level of achievement will be necessary for you to secure the career you want or for entrance into a specific college?"* Then help the student to plan backward. If your students have unrealistic career goals, such as becoming professional athletes, top models or rock stars, point out how unlikely it is that this will happen, and remind them that good coaches always have more than one game plan. Then encourage them, in the same way, to have more than one game plan for their life! (See *Becoming an Achiever* by Carolyn Coil, Pieces of Learning, for more suggestions about helping students with goal setting.)

2. Have high, firm expectations of students which teachers, students and parents agree to.

High expectations are of almost no use unless everyone agrees they are important and works to attain them. One important element of having high expectations for students is to also have consistent and enforceable consequences when they do not meet the expectations. This does not have to be a punitive action. Instead, the consequence may be additional study time, more help in an academic area, more review or remediation, etc.

3. Show your students real world connections and the long-term benefits of acquiring high academic skills.

Go on field trips to see how highly educated people work in the world of business and industry, invite a variety of professionals who have high academic skills as guest speakers, and use mentors who will challenge your students beyond grade level work to function more as professionals do in the *real world*. Often the biggest impact can come from young professionals just beginning their careers who can reflect on the importance of education in their lives.

4. Expose your top students to other top students throughout the district or state via academic competitions, academic fairs, club affiliations, etc.

Discuss their achievements compared to others of equal ability and challenge them to be the top of the top.

5. Explain why education is important for the sake of learning itself, not only as a step toward a career.

In the early days of American history, discussion about education's benefits centered on its public, democratic and social benefits. Thomas Jefferson was one of the most influential proponents of this view, and his thoughts shaped public attitudes about education during our first decades as a nation. Today, most of the discussions about the value of education involve its economic benefits, the ability to compete in a global marketplace, and as a way to reduce crime, poverty, the number of people in prison, etc. While these benefits are important, we must remind our students of other less tangible rewards. Education can produce life long learners who appreciate the arts, literature and culture and who can be more caring compassionate people with strong interpersonal and intra personal skills. Emphasize these advantages to your students.

Fear of Failure

Samantha is considered the class clown. Everyone laughs at her antics and tells her she drives the teacher nuts. She is a source of amusement to her classmates, but she creates lots of problems for her teacher. Samantha's disruptions result in everyone learning less. Underneath her jolly exterior, Samantha is unsure of herself and has a tremendous fear of failure. She often clowns around to avoid doing the required work. *"If I do nothing,"* she figures, *"then I can't do it wrong."*

James is a perfectionist with unrealistic expectations of himself and others. He is a highly able student but seems to have built a wall around himself which is difficult to penetrate. He is a teacher pleaser who does not like risk taking or challenges. Particularly in front of the class, James seems to pull back. He fears competition with his peers. After nearly every assignment, he compares his results with others and if his is not the best in the class, he regards it as a failure.

As we can see from the two very different students described above, fear of failure is a complex phenomenon. Signs of a fear of failure may include tears, refusal to complete assigned tasks, perfectionism, a refusal to participate in classroom activities, procrastination, nonconformity and creative excuses for not doing work.

Some students learn to accept the failure label and get some of their identity from it. Others seem not to care about failure and verbally brush it off. These students seem unable to accept help. Yet they are often the ones failure bothers the most, thus they are the least able to deal with it in a positive and proactive way.

Some students will not respond unless they are 100% certain of the answer. Therefore, with these students, when the teacher asks a risky question, he often gets a rebellious reaction or a response that indicates they can't think or can't come up with any creative ideas.

Failure is a spiral that continually goes downward. After the first few experiences with failure in school, many students fear more failure. Often an attitude covers up this fear and sounds like, *"I could care less,"* but the cause of such an attitude is usually fear of continued failure with no way to save face.

Somehow schools do not give students the message that failure and mistakes can be positive learning experiences. Rarely in a school situation do we celebrate or articulate what we have learned from our mistakes. Instead, failure is something to be hidden with false phrases encouraging self-esteem or glossed over as we go on to the next concept or unit of study.

Yet many famous and successful people have been considered failures at some point in their lives. Consider the following examples:

- Abraham Lincoln ran for office eight times and was only elected three times.

- John Grisham received 24 rejection slips before his first book was published.

- The Army rejected hopeful recruit Teddy Roosevelt which prompted him to organize the Rough Riders.

- When Winston Churchill was 16 years old, his teacher wrote on his report card, "This student shows a conspicuous lack of success."

- Thomas Edison tried hundreds of filaments that would not function before inventing one that worked in his electric light bulb.

- 409 Cleaner was invented on the 409th try. 408 formulas for this cleaning solution were failures.

NOTES

Learning from Mistakes and Failures: Strategies for Student Success

1. Grade positively instead of negatively.

Student assessment is a major reason for a fear of failure in school. Most teachers feel that grading student work is necessary. When you give grades, give points for what has been done correctly rather than taking points off for incorrect responses. This puts the emphasis on what was done right rather than on what was done wrong.

2. Encourage individual self-evaluation and self-assessment.

Help each of your students reflect upon their own goals, successes and failures in learning. Students with a fear of failure benefit from having individual goals so they can't compare their performance with others. Questions they should ask themselves include: *What did I do well? What could I do better next time? What strategies can I use to improve my work?*

3. Use nonthreatening group self-assessment.

While students with a fear of failure do not benefit from being compared with others, they do benefit from assessing a group effort or process they were part of. Use the reproducible form on the next page for student group self-assessment.

WORKING TOGETHER
IN A COOPERATIVE GROUP
Self-Assessment Guidelines for Students

✎ *Rate your group according to the following scale:*

1 = We didn't do this at all   2 = We need a lot of help in this
3 = We did well with this   4 = We were outstanding in this

Commitment to Purpose   Group Rating _____
Interest in task
Motivation to complete assignment
Followed directions

Work Process   Group Rating _____
Everyone participated
We didn't waste time
Ideas built on one another

Decision Making   Group Rating _____
Looked for solutions all could accept
Followed orderly process in making decisions
Decisions were not forced on some people

Communication   Group Rating _____
Listened to all suggestions
We stayed on task in discussions
Our talking did not disturb the class

Creativity   Group Rating _____
Considered new ways of doing things
Brainstormed ideas
No put downs for different thinking

Conflict   Group Rating _____
Established rules for dealing with conflict
Avoided personal attacks
Examined different points of view

Leadership   Group Rating _____
Group decided on leadership tasks and roles
Everyone took some responsibility
Group leader was fair to all

Group Members: _____

NOTES

4. Stress the benefits of trial and error in learning.

Remind your students that an eraser on a pencil and the **delete** key on a computer exist for corrections! When approximately 10,000 experiments with a storage battery failed to produce results, Thomas Edison once remarked, *"I have not failed. I've just found 10,000 ways that won't work."* Our students need to have a similar attitude!

5. Guide students to see different perspectives or answers instead of concentrating on the one correct answer.

Emphasize open-ended questions with multiple responses. Aim for a balance of these questions along with the factual questions with one right answer. A typical classroom activity or lesson often limits thinking. When we insist on finding the one right answer, we are ignoring how people actually learn. Human beings have learned new information for centuries by trying out new things using a myriad of options. When standardized or teacher-created tests always focus on students getting the right answer, this does not encourage students to engage in the higher level thinking they need to use in solving real problems throughout their lives. (See *Questioning Makes the Difference* and *Active Questioning* by Nancy Johnson, Pieces of Learning, to learn more about creative questioning techniques.)

6. Encourage a step-by-step approach to positive risk-taking.

People who take risks in a positive way generally have developed the skill of risk-taking slowly. Encourage your students, especially perfectionists, to begin by taking one very small risk. Trying something new and risky will be more successful and less terrifying this way! Talk about the difference between taking risks that can result in something positive and risky behavior which will only have negative results in the end. We do not want to encourage students to take foolish risks or engage in negative risk-taking behavior!

7. Discuss the worst case scenario and then go beyond it.

When presented with a new idea or task, many students who have a fear of failure immediately think of the worst possible thing that could happen if they tried to do the task and didn't succeed! Encourage these students to verbalize or write out their worst case scenarios but don't stop there. Have students look at the end of their worst case scenario and then ask, *"What would happen next?"* This usually gives students a new perspective. Even if the worst thing happens (which it probably won't), life will go on, learning will take place, and generally things will return to normal.

8. Assess and teach basic academic skills - don't assume your students already know them.

Find a way to assess academic skill levels before you begin instruction on a unit or topic. This way, you can tell which students don't need the instruction and can compact out of this part of the curriculum and which students need direct instruction or remediation to succeed. Encourage achievement in all students by differentiating your curriculum to meet individual student needs.

NOTES

NOTES

9. Assess your students' abilities in organization and study skills.

Some of your students may fear failure not because they are unable to master the academic content but because they don't know how to organize their work and their time, or because they have not developed good study skills. Be intentional about teaching these skills rather than saying your students *should* know them!

10. Be a role model for coping with failure, showing that after a failure one can recover and go on.

All of us have discovered ways to cope with and learn from our own mistakes and failures. Yet we generally do not share this with our students. Somehow we think it seems best if we keep these things hidden. Take some time to consider how you have used your own failures as opportunities to grow and learn. Decide which of these you could share with your students to show them some positive results of failures. Use this as a discussion starter for how they can use mistakes as a means of motivation and encouragement.

11. Use motivational quotations about failure as starters for journal writing, short stories, creative writing, reflective thinking, etc.

Many quotations about failure can serve to encourage your students. Use the ones on the next page as starters. Encourage your students to find more.

12. Have students share examples of people who have overcome fear and anxiety in literature, films and current events.

Use the worksheet on page 74 as a guide.

Quotes About Failure

- *Failure is the opportunity to begin again more intelligently - Thomas Jefferson*

- *Failure means you need to try a different strategy - It doesn't mean you are dumb!*

- *You almost always encounter failure on the road to success.*

- *I have not failed. I've just found 10,000 ways that won't work. - Thomas Edison*

- *Always bear in mind that your own resolution to succeed is more important than any other thing. - Abraham Lincoln*

- *Failure is a great teacher. Only those people who try run the risk of failure. The main choice that each person makes in life is at what level to fail. - Zell Miller, Former Governor of Georgia*

AN OVERCOMER

A person who has overcome stress, fear or failure

Name of person _____

Obstacle(s) overcome _____

_____

_____

How it happened _____

_____

_____

Source of this information _____

_____

_____

I will share this information with my classmates in the following way

_____

_____

How this could be a model for my life _____

_____

My plan of action

_____

_____

_____

Reproducible

Taking Responsibility

> *The teacher did not explain . . . did not give me enough time . . . would not help me . . . was going too fast.*
>
> *The kid in the chair next to me is bothering me . . . touching me . . . took my things . . . is talking about my mama.*
>
> *I don't have my homework because I didn't know I was supposed to do it . . . the printer on my computer broke . . . I had to go to soccer practice . . . my dog ate it.*
>
> *You know my little son/daughter just didn't have enough time to do the work . . . left his/her homework on the kitchen table . . . was with his/her grandmother last night . . . needs an easier assignment . . . is bored in your class so he/she didn't do the assignment.*

Excuses, excuses, excuses!! Teachers hear hundreds of them. Students need to learn to take responsibility for their own behaviors and work. Many students depend on other students to carry the load to achieve success. Kids manipulate the situation and then blame the other person - a teacher, parent, classmate, the environment they live in, outside influences, etc.

Too many parents are quick to back off when their kids object or complain. They bail them out of difficult situations, make excuses and are quick to give in when the going gets tough. Parents and teachers must look at the best interests of the child in the **long-term** and not just seek the easiest **short-term** solution. Encouraging a child does not mean giving into his or her every whim or being talked out of giving a punishment or consequence the child deserves.

NOTES

Encouraging Responsibility:
Strategies for Success

1. List clear expectations to the children and parents.

Being responsible is difficult if one does not know exactly what the expectations are. Often educators know exactly what they expect and think they have communicated this to parents and students. Do not assume that a signed form listing rules and expectations means your parents and students really understand what you expect. Encouraging achievement often means reiterating expectations and explaining them repeatedly.

2. Teach and model responsible behavior.

Don't just **talk the talk;** you must also **walk the walk.** This is a saying I heard often during my childhood, and I think it has a great deal of relevance today. We want our children to learn responsibility, yet many adults do not act responsibly. Make sure you personally take responsibility for your actions, and when you do, point this out to children.

3. Be honest with your students and their parents. Don't beat around the bush.

One sign of responsible behavior is the ability to **tell it like it is** without being rude or insensitive. Teachers do not like being the bearers of bad news to parents. Parents often feel they are not getting the full story from the school. Be honest about your students and their specific abilities and problems. This is one way for everyone to learn to work together and take responsibility for solving whatever problems there are.

4. Allow children to be part of making decisions which will affect their lives.

Too often adults make all of the major decisions and then tell the child what is going to happen. Then we wonder why the child makes such poor decisions and takes no responsibility for his actions or behavior. As much as possible, include the child in discussions where decisions are being made about him. As a player in the decision making process, the child will also feel more responsibility about the decisions being made.

5. Encourage parents to assign daily chores for their children to do at home.

I observed one student in a classroom who was particularly self-confident, full of suggestions, able to debate and stand up for her point of view and could organize her thoughts and work. I discovered she had learned these skills not in school but at home where she had significant responsibility for doing chores. There was a time when most children did chores at home. Fewer kids have that kind of responsibility today, but the ones who do often stand out as achievers in the classroom. Doing chores teaches children to see a task through from start to finish and to see their own value in their home, classroom and community.

6. Design a *Student Self-Assessment Form for students who have taken responsibility for their own work and actions. Have students complete it and take it home to their parents.*

An example is on the next page.

NOTES

Student Self-Assessment Form

Name _____

Date _____

My work today included _____

_____

_____

_____

_____

I made my own decisions by_____

_____

_____

_____

_____

I took responsibility for _____

_____

_____

_____

_____

Reproducible

THE ROLE OF THE FAMILY

The Role of the Family

> Jamal's mother was trying to hold back the tears. Ten-year-old Jamal had come home with another poor progress report and she could see things were not going well for him in school. The problem was, he was disruptive and disobedient at home as well. She felt upset, overwhelmed and hopeless about the situation and wondered if one more punishment would really do any good. *"I never knew it would be so hard to be a parent,"* she said to herself. *"What will happen when he's a teenager?"*

Parental attitudes, worries and concerns, and family situations and problems have a tremendous impact on student achievement. Like Jamal's mother described above, many parents are at a loss about what to do for and with their children. In this chapter, we explore some problems parents face and some things parents do which discourage achievement. We also look at many ideas and strategies which suggest countless ways parents and teachers can work together to encourage student achievement and success.

Parental Attitudes Which May <u>Discourage</u> Achievement

• **Parents who are unhappy in the parental role.**

Some parents never wanted to be parents in the first place and others did not realize what a huge job it was when they decided to have a baby. Other parents are not much more than children themselves. Parents who are not happy or comfortable in their role as parents are poor guides for their children and often do not have the skills to point the way toward achievement and school success.

• **High levels of anxiety**

Parenting is one of the most difficult jobs in the world. Parents who are overwhelmed and stressed out due to the responsibilities associated with being a parent, or due to other problems and concerns, often transfer these anxious feelings to their children. This, in turn, makes the children more stressed and worried and less likely to do well in school.

• **Not firm or consistent in setting expectations and standards**

Parents must be firm in what they expect, what their rules are, and what boundaries exist for their children. Parents who say one thing one minute and something else the next, or who make threats or set unrealistic consequences for behavior but never carry them out, lose the respect of their children. The children tune them out and develop the attitude that rules and expectations are meaningless. They often transfer this attitude to the school setting which may result in poor school performance.

- **Negative attitudes toward education; school not a priority**

Parents who put a low priority on success in school or who verbalize negative attitudes about the value of an education, the abilities of the principal or teacher, or about the organization of the school itself discourage their children in terms of even trying to do well in school. Other parents seem to have negative attitudes when they do not return school phone calls, miss conferences or blame the teacher when their child does poorly in school. Parental attitudes like these provide tremendous disincentives for children who already do not work hard at school.

- **Not supportive of a child's abilities**

Some children show great promise in the first few years of school. They pay attention, do their work, participate in class, show creativity and have varied interests. Parents who negate this type of child, who will not follow up and encourage their child's special interest areas outside school, or who have the attitude that doing schoolwork is a waste of time will ultimately discourage their child, even a child with many skills and abilities and great potential, to be successful in school and in life.

- **Overly enthusiastic and helpful with a child's assignments**

An overly enthusiastic and involved parent might be one who comes to school, follows the child to class, cleans out his locker and waits in the hall for him at the end of the day. It might be a parent who requires that every book be brought home daily or one who takes over the work of a child's school project so that the finished product far exceeds the child's ability. These actions discourage achievement because the message to the child is, *"You can't do this well enough on your own, so I must help you. To be #1 you need my help."* As a result, the child may feel discouraged and inadequate and will have a hard time developing independent learning skills. Parents need to recognize there is a balance between not enough involvement with their kids and too much involvement. Both extremes can create problems!

- **Counter identification**

Similar to the overly enthusiastic parent, this parent overidentifies with the same sex child, almost living his or her life through the child. Typical examples are the Little League father who is mentally and emotionally *up to bat* every time his son swings at a ball and the *dancing school mom* who forces her daughter into dancing lessons and recitals. Sometimes this type of parental behavior results in children who are stressed-out overachievers. However, other children may say to themselves, *"I could never do it as well as he/she wants me to, so I won't try at all."* These children become discouraged underachievers.

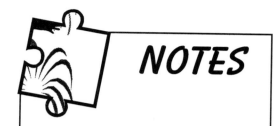

NOTES

Strategies for Teachers: Working with Parents to Encourage Achievement

1. Collaborate and brainstorm ideas with parents.

Help parents develop strategies for handling and working with their child or for solving a specific problem the child may have. Help them in finding solutions and strategies for dealing with discipline and health problems and with their own vocational, educational and household skills.

2. Help parents to develop practical, related, predetermined consequences and realistic expectations for their child.

Show parents the value of imposing immediate consequences on their child rather than having punishments which don't begin until several days after the bad behavior occurs. Emphasize follow through. Explain that making excuses for the child, giving in when he or she complains, whines or cries and rationalizing his or her behavior are counterproductive.

3. Have a conference involving parents, teacher, counselor, student and an administrator to develop a plan of action to encourage and increase achievement.

Discuss appropriate interventions to help the family. If needed, suggest parent, student, or family counseling and provide information about outside community resources and services parents can use. Refer parents to a counselor or social service agency as required.

NOTES

4. Organize parent involvement programs, parenting courses and workshops to educate parents about their child's needs.

Give parents training and materials to help them stimulate their child's cognitive development and nurture their child's emotional development.

5. Develop strategies which will help parents let the child take responsibility for his or her own behavior and actions.

For example, have students sign for their progress reports and report cards, documenting that they did receive them and that they have the responsibility to take them home and give them to their parents.

6. Encourage parents to help their kids develop skills in self-sufficiency including how to pack their own lunches, clean their rooms, put away toys, wash clothes and manage/organize their time.

Parents who do these things for their children do them no favor in the end. Many parents are not willing to take the time to teach and enforce these skills, finding it takes less time to do them themselves. Eventually, however, the extra time it takes to develop such skills is well worth it.

7. Deal with the Parent Rescue Syndrome on a school-wide basis.

Have a school-wide phone call policy not allowing calls except in case of an emergency. Come to a consensus at each grade level regarding how many times per week, month or grading period parents are allowed to bring forgotten lunches, notebooks, homework, notes, etc. to school.

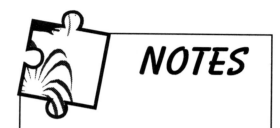

NOTES

8. Maintain contact between home and school.

Keep parents informed through parent conferences and interviews, home visits, newsletters, e-mail messages, automated voice mail, student portfolios, notes and phone calls. Use any technology available to both you and the parent to aid in home-school communication. Create a system for regular communication between home and school with consistent expectations for the student, parent and teacher. Let parents know you value their input and efforts, their comments and concerns. Make them feel needed, wanted and appreciated.

9. Help the parents develop a realistic view of their child and the school.

Use checklists and observation logs to document the child's behavior, strengths and weaknesses. Encourage parents to come and observe your class or help as a volunteer in your classroom and throughout the school. In this way they will see their child in the school setting and will understand more about what goes on at school. (See *Involving Parents in Schools* by Kathy Steele, Pieces of Learning.)

10. Encourage parents to find or organize after school tutoring outside the school environment in places such as childcare centers, the Y, churches or boys' and girls' clubs.

Sometimes helping their own children with academic skills or homework is difficult for parents. Many civic or community groups, churches and other organizations are open to the idea of helping children in this way. However, it often takes an interested advocate such as a parent to get the program going. Facilitating such a program, which could benefit many children, is sometimes exactly what works to channel the energy and enthusiasm of a parent who has been overly interested in her own child.

Family Situations Which Make Achievement More Difficult

- **Family instability**

The American family has gone through profound changes in the past 30 years. Family structures have changed, more women work, families move from place to place with greater frequency, and downsizing or corporate restructuring and mergers make continual employment less certain. Divorce and remarriage are commonplace. Some kids live with grandparents while others see a series of live-in boyfriends or girlfriends come in and out of their homes. Others move and change schools several times in one school year! These conditions can create a climate of family instability which serves to discourage achievement.

- **Power struggle between mother and father**

Playing one parent against another is a favorite game of the manipulative child who knows his parents do not get along. These may be divorced parents, parents who live in the same household but never communicate, or parents who argue constantly. Parents who provide a united front in dealing with their children (regardless of personal problems) are more likely to encourage their children and to have children who succeed in school.

- **Indifference, neglect, no time for communication**

In many families, life is full of too many activities. Time is at a premium. With both parents working, some children are left to wake up and get to school on their own. Many children rarely eat a meal with their parents or have time for evening conversation or a story. This results in little or no communication. One study showed that the average parent talks to his or her child only 12 minutes per day! Is it any wonder children turn to the TV for conversation and entertainment? These factors discourage a child's school achievement.

- **Having more power, responsibility or freedom than the child knows how to use**

Some parents don't discuss expectations, rules or boundaries with their children, but they require these children to assume adult responsibilities without the maturity or necessary knowledge. In such cases, there is little or no parental supervision and the child often assumes he can do whatever he wants. This independence and freedom without commensurate skills in responsible behavior is a recipe for underachievement in school.

- **No positive role models**

Children learn how to act and behave by watching others. A role model is someone a child can look up to and hope to be like. Unfortunately, many children are only exposed to negative role models, both in their homes and in the world of celebrities, often as presented by the media. When children have no positive role models, they learn negative ways of dealing with life. This discourages achievement and does not bode well for success in school.

NOTES

Strategies to Encourage and Involve Students, Parents, and Families

1. Assign family discussion as a part of homework assignments.

Current events, family memories, and favorite foods or books are some possible topics as well as discussion focusing on the subject, topic or unit being studied in class. Ask students to summarize the discussion in a short journal entry or in a learner's log.

2. Assign an interview of parents or grandparents.

What better way to learn interview skills than to interview one's parents or grandparents? Teach interviewing techniques, helping students to formulate appropriate questions. They can show the results of the interview in many ways, such as a written log, a radio show on audio tape, or a scrapbook with illustrations.

3. Invite parents to take tests with their children.

Plan a take-home test specifically designed to be done as a joint effort by parents and children. Encourage discussion of answers and stipulate whether they can use books and other resources. This type of test is a fantastic learning tool!

4. Create a Family Final Exam.

This final exam can cover the basic information learned in your grade or subject or it can focus more on open-ended questions which have no right or wrong answers but do require higher level thinking skills. The **Leading Questions** from an **Encounter Lesson** (see pages 151-152) provide a great format for a **Family Final Exam.**

NOTES

5. Ask students to write a humorous family anecdote or story about a family member.

Be sure to emphasize humor (not sarcasm) in this activity. Laughter is part of the glue that binds families together, and often funny stories provide a way to link generations of family members together.

6. Guide students in making a Month of Memories Calendar.

Provide each of your students with a blank monthly calendar. During each day of the month, they are to write a special memory about a family member or something that happened at home on that day.

7. Give parents suggestions for family field trips.

Holidays, vacations and weekends provide the perfect opportunity for families to do things together. Generate a list of inexpensive and educational places families could visit no more than an hour or two from your school or town. Include potential educational activities and experiences that could be completed at each location.

8. Talk to parents individually about finding time to be with their children.

Time is the most precious commodity for most parents and the thing they have the least of. Finding more time to be with one's children is a matter of setting priorities, as no one can add more hours to the day! Talk to parents about making their children their first priority.

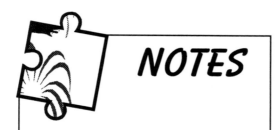

NOTES

9. Organize booster clubs for parents which emphasize academics.

Athletic teams and music organizations have had booster clubs for years. These clubs do fundraisers, organize events and advocate or promote the importance of their activity. Start a science booster club for parents whose children are particularly interested in science or a booster club for budding writers. Such clubs can generate lots of interest in academics!

10. Have a Fun Day to involve parents and teachers in an informal setting.

An unstructured day at a park, an evening spent doing arts and crafts or exploring technology, and a potluck supper followed by family games are examples of ways to get to know parents informally. Some of your most valuable insights about your students will come from these types of informal events.

11. Assign optional interdisciplinary family projects involving language arts, math, science, visual/performing arts and social studies.

Design some projects you assign to be done just by the student. Others can only be done at home, sometimes with the help of parents. Design some family projects which will involve parents and students in learning. (See the individualized lesson plans in *Teaching Tools for the 21st Century* by Carolyn Coil, Pieces of Learning, for examples of family projects.)

12. Involve families in setting goals for their children and for the family as a whole.

"You never reach the goal if you don't know where you're headed," an astute 4th grader once told me. He was referring to football goals, but his

observation is accurate for all of life. Families encourage achievement in all areas when they set goals together and help the children set individual goals.

13. Use successful family members as role models for your students. This is particularly important in close-knit ethnic communities.

Family members within your community may be your best resource. Children often look to celebrities as role models, but being like a celebrity is a farfetched dream for most. A more realistic (and often more positive) role model may be found in the house next door! Find these role models in your community and involve them in the life of your school and your classroom.

14. Share family activity information with parents.

Parents may need suggestions concerning how to plan and how to provide beneficial activities for their children. This is why they often turn to organized recreational activities in the community or sit their kids in front of the TV. Use the reproducible **Family Fun Time** handout found on the next two pages to give parents suggestions for fun and educational activities to do with their children.

15. Discuss ideas with parents about how they can help to encourage achievement at home.

Use the reproducible handouts at the end of this chapter to give parents a list of suggested strategies.

FAMILY FUN TIME

10 Inexpensive, Enjoyable and Educational Activities
Parents Can Plan and Do With Their Kids

1. Backyard Camp-out

A sheet thrown over a card table or a more elaborate tent and sleeping bag provide the basics for camping in the backyard. Whether camping is done for an hour, an evening or overnight, it teaches many important skills. Camping involves organizational skills to plan the event, math skills for measuring out the campsite and preparing food, language skills when kids tell ghost stories or keep journals of the event, science skills to observe nature, and musical skills for singing and making up new camp songs.

2. Monster Storytelling

Gather **monster body parts** from ordinary household items and food such as grapes (eyeballs), melon (head), cold spaghetti (brains), a twig with several branches (fingers), etc. Sit in a circle in a darkened room with eyes closed. Pass each *body part* around. Each person has to guess what part of the monster it is and make up a story about it. Great for developing creativity and language skills.

3. Bottle Art

Buy colored sand or construction paper at a local discount or arts and crafts store. Use clean empty bottles or jars for containers. Have your children cut the paper into small pieces. Then they can make designs by putting layers of the paper or sand into the bottles. This teaches skills in visual perception, creativity, and estimating.

4. Restaurant Ratings Report Card

Take your kids to one restaurant per week for six weeks for a special treat or meal. Before going to the first restaurant, each child must list 10 things on which he or she will judge the food and restaurant. For example: The hamburger is as big as the bun, or the fries were crispy, or the food was worth the money. Each item will get a **report card** rating or grade. They make a new list before going to each restaurant. At the end of six weeks, have each child write a restaurant review about his favorite local restaurant. Send this to your local newspaper or the restaurant manager. This teaches higher level thinking skills and writing skills.

5. Family Tree

Tell your children to gather several twigs and branches of various sizes (not too big). Have them arrange these on a large piece of posterboard to make a family tree. Then glue or tape them onto the posterboard. The number of branches on the family tree will depend on how large your family is. Next, have them trace a leaf on construction paper for each family member. Write the name of a family member on the paper leaf. Cut it out and tape it on the tree. Challenge them to find out more about your family history and add leaves to the tree. This teaches organizational skills, visual arts, and communication skills.

Reproducible

6. Family Map

Get a map of the United States or a world map which you can hang on a wall or bulletin board somewhere in your house. Have your kids find the birthplace of family members including parents, aunts, uncles, grandparents, and great-grandparents, and place each name on that location on the map. Broaden this activity to include neighbors, friends, favorite TV stars, etc. This teaches geography and map skills.

7. Challenge the Weatherman

Have your child make a chart with four columns. At the top of Column 1 write **Date**, Column 2 **Weatherman Prediction**, column 3 **My Prediction** and column 4 **Actual Weather.** Your child should watch or listen to the local weather once each day and write down the weatherman's prediction and his or her prediction for the next day. He should also observe and record the actual weather for each day and any unusual weather patterns or phenomena. At the end of a week, have your child figure out the percentages of correct predictions. This teaches skills in record keeping, scientific observation and math.

8. 'Hop 'n Think Scotch'

Make a hopscotch game but put categories in each square in addition to numbers. Categories could include Favorite Books, Types of Trees, Ways to Say 100, States, Cities or Countries beginning with a certain letter, Multiples of 6, etc. A score can be kept with one point for each different thing that they name. Increase the number of things to be named in a category as the children's skills improve. This teaches memory, categorizing and thinking skills, balance and dexterity. It is a great way for active children to review for a test.

9. Create a Board Game

Help your child create a game of "Neighborhood Monopoly" or family favorites "Candyland" or "Clue" with his or her own set of characters. Adapt and personalize any board game. Even better, your child can devise his or her own game, game cards and rules. All your child needs is posterboard, markers, lots of good ideas and time! This teaches problem solving, math skills and how to develop workable rules.

10. Real World Role Play

Playing is one way kids get to know what the *real world is* like. Perhaps they would like to be the teacher and play school with younger children. Or they could set up a bank complete with play money and a cardboard ATM Machine. Children can make a supermarket with empty boxes and cans from the grocery store - as long as they are clean! In pretending to be a newspaper reporter, your child could write a paper, have it copied and give it away to friends. If you have a video camera, several kids might want to produce their own TV show. Each place from the *real world* teaches different skills, but generally they will develop skills in working with others, categorizing, math and money, writing, spelling and organization.

Challenge the Weatherman

Date	Weatherman Prediction	My Prediction	Actual Weather

Unusual Observations:

Percent of correct predictions: weatherman _____

Percent of correct predictions: me _____

Reproducible

Sample Restaurant Ratings Report Card

Give each of the items listed below a report card grade. Be sure you can give reasons for the grades you give!

Items to be Graded   **Grade**

Tables were clean   _____

Bathroom was clean   _____

Not expensive   _____

Food was healthy and low in fat   _____

Many food choices   _____

The food tasted good   _____

Quick service   _____

Second helpings of drinks were free   _____

Kids were welcome here   _____

Had a toy, treat, freebie or contest   _____

Comments:

Encouraging Achievement: Homework and Studying

"Say not 'When I have leisure I will study'; you may not have leisure." - The Mishnah

Homework has the potential to be the most important link between home and school. It provides the means through which parents can keep up with what their child is studying in school. Homework can help children learn better. Doing assigned homework consistently improves grades and makes children better readers. It also teaches children responsibility and self-discipline.

Unfortunately, homework can also be the biggest battleground between parents and children. An ideal homework situation occurs when the parents are at home doing their own studying or reading while homework is being done. Parents may take the role as guides or assistants with homework, but never more than that. A parent should never do the homework for the child! Notify the teacher if the child continually struggles with homework assignments. Encourage students to ask the teacher when they do not understand the homework! This kind of problem may need special help and collaborative planning by the parent and the teacher.

All schools need a homework policy. Students should not have hours and hours of homework nightly. Teachers should assign homework to reinforce and extend those things studied in school and to give each child the opportunity to enrich his learning in a specific topic or interest area. Students should have some type of feedback about their homework from their teachers, though every homework assignment need not receive a grade.

Encouraging Achievement through Homework: Suggestions for Teachers

- *Make sure all children understand their assignments before leaving your classroom for the day.*
- *Follow through on homework assignments and give some type of feedback.*
- *Have a daily homework policy so that everyone knows the expectations every day.*
- *Have a procedure to facilitate communication with parents about homework.*

Encouraging Achievement through Homework: Suggestions for Parents

- *Set a study time each afternoon or evening where everyone in the house reads and studies.*
- *Make one area of the house the study area and have all necessary supplies in one place. This may include encyclopedias, dictionaries, a computer, paper, pencils, pens, markers, etc.*
- *Don't ask your child, "Do you have any homework tonight?" If there is no assigned homework, a child always has something he can study or something he can read during the scheduled study time.*
- *Allow classical music to play softly in the background during study time. This type of music, especially pieces by Mozart, seems to enhance learning.*

Strategies for Parents to Encourage Achievement
Developing Self-Esteem, Motivation, and Responsibility

1. Find some positive characteristics about your child and emphasize these. Spending all of your time pointing out the things your child is doing wrong is easy. Try to mention the good things 10 times as often as the bad.

2. Don't use **put-downs** or sarcasm when correcting your child. Sarcastic remarks are very tempting, especially toward teenagers. Resist the temptation! Sarcasm can create wounds for a lifetime.

3. Avoid the role of **rescuer**. Let your child experience the consequences of forgetting a note, homework or lunch money. He or she will learn from this experience!

4. Discourage perfectionism. Emphasize what your child has learned, even if he or she made mistakes. If your child brings home a school paper or test with a low grade, look first at the items he or she got right. When looking at incorrect answers, ask what your child has now learned about the question.

5. Be aware of times your child is trying to manipulate you. Children who learn they can talk their way out of anything, or manipulate their parents into doing everything the way they want, learn how to be little dictators and how to be very sneaky.

6. Be aware of your child's areas of intense interest and build on them. Use success in these areas to build success in school. Encourage participation and learning in these interest areas even when your child is doing poorly in school. Don't take away the area of interest your child has as a punishment for not doing well in school. This is counterproductive!

7. Work with your child on setting goals. Short-term goals are important. Remember, even a month is a long time from a child's point of view!

8. Don't use threats but have reasonable and enforceable consequences for misbehavior. If you need to take away a privilege, make the punishment fit the crime and make sure you can enforce it.

9. Collect **success stories** of people who are self-motivated. Look for similar characteristics in your child and point these out.

10. Help your child create external motivators. Instead of giving rewards to your child for doing something right or accomplishing a goal, have the child think of a way to reward himself or herself after the task is completed. This teaches **deferred gratification.**

11. Don't overload your child with activities. Choose to omit some activities so the family has time at home together.

Strategies for Parents to Encourage Achievement
Developing Good Study Skills

1. Make a plan for organizing the study environment and study time at home. Your child should be involved in making the plan so he or she knows exactly what is expected.

2. Help your child in developing organizational skills. Many children need help in knowing how to organize. Work on one organizational skill at a time. Your child will be less overwhelmed than trying to do everything at once.

3. Make a checklist of materials needed at school and materials needed at home. Post this in an obvious place, such as the bathroom mirror or inside the car.

4. Design a system where you periodically check your child's notebooks. Have your child bring home notebooks or folders regularly so that he can share what he is learning in school, what assignments he is working on, etc.

5. Promote a love of reading in your home. Turn off the TV and have a reading night at least once a week! Use your imagination and creativity to make the most inviting place in your home the **Reading Area.**

6. Work on improving memory techniques. Look for games that require a good memory. List all the techniques you and your child can think of which help to remember things.

7. Help your child make flash cards, mindmaps, charts, lists or drawings to learn key terms or facts.

8. Be aware of a drop in grades or achievement test scores. Find out why this is happening before the problem gets severe.

9. Discover your child's academic weaknesses. Brainstorm ways to make learning fun in these areas.

10. Learn about **learning styles.** Help your child recognize his/her strong and weak learning styles. Compare this with your own.

11. Set aside a **study time** in your home **every night.** Parents should allow no activities other than studying (assigned homework or studying a topic of individual interest) during study time.

12. Be a life long learner yourself. Continue to learn new things, share these things with your child, and model the learning process.

13. Encourage your child to teach things he/she knows to someone younger or to someone older. This gives a great sense of accomplishment.

Reproducible

DEALING WITH CHILDREN'S STRESS

Dealing with Children's Stress

Janine's mom is worried about her. Janine is considered a good student in her 10th grade class and is involved in several extracurricular activities at school. However, lately it seems she is getting very little sleep and on most days she just seems exhausted. Yet with the pressure to succeed so intense and the competition to get into college so stiff, Janine seems to think she is not doing enough. *"How could childhood have become so stressful?"* her mom wonders.

Rob wakes up with a stomachache or headache almost every morning. He doesn't do as well in school as his parents would like and it seems to him they keep putting more and more pressure on him. At school the teacher keeps talking about the importance of the up-coming standardized tests. Rob's stomach goes into knots when he hears that. He would just like to pull the covers over his head and never go to school again.

Stressed out kids are everywhere in our society. Like Janine and Rob described above, their stresses are multiple and seem to be unending. Too many activities, test anxiety, high expectations, problems at home, parental pressure, pressure put on oneself, fear of failure, perfectionism - these and many more cause children to be stressed. Surprisingly, parents generally rate their children as very happy and not stressed at all. We live under the myth of the happy, carefree childhood, but this is not always the case.

Dr. Hans Selye, long considered a pioneer in stress research, defines stress as the non-specific response of the body to any demand made on it. He states that the optimal level of stress for any individual is the *"highest level of activity that is pleasant for you."* Some people need to lower, while others need to raise, their level of stress, either by slowing down or by adding more spark or excitement to their lives. Some stress, called **eustress**, is good. It keeps you lively and alert. But too much stress, particularly bad stress or **distress**, is a killer according to medical experts.

With too much stress, children and adults alike tend to be irritable, exhausted, over-whelmed, unable to make decisions quickly and prone to illness. With too little stress, people are bored, tired, frustrated, unhappy, and again prone to illness. With just the right balance, we can be happy, creative, motivated, productive and healthy. Helping our students find this balance is an important factor in encouraging their achievement.

Throughout their school years, students seem to experience times of stress on both ends of the spectrum. Sometimes they have too little positive stress and are bored and tired, saying they have nothing to do. In fact, they may do nothing because of doubts or worry about how to cope or how to look cool.

At other times they experience high stress due to test anxiety, accompanied by an inability to memorize and comprehend assigned work. Many children feel a great deal of parental pressure and often the number of activities they must do and the number of external expectations overwhelms them.

Boys in particular experience stress when they are uneasy about their status in relation to their peers and when they are involved in unhealthy competition. Girls seem more concerned about relationships with others and can get their feelings hurt easily when group or individual friendships go awry. Girls are twice as likely as boys to be depressed and four times as likely to commit suicide. They also tend to have more negative feelings about their bodies and appearance.

Common threats and stressors for students in school:

- detention

- low grades

- loss of school privileges

- embarrassment

- feeling dumb

- not understanding English well

- unrealistic deadlines

- humiliation

- sarcasm

- being bullied

- conflict with teachers and/or classmates

- overcrowded, dirty or messy classrooms

- excess noise or temperature

Excess stress and threat in the school environment may be the single greatest factor in discouraging achievement in school. A typical school day for any child will have its share of stresses in the form of disappointments, scores that are lower than expected, friends that don't seem to like you, teachers who yell at you, lost homework, a pop quiz, etc.

Often these stressors impair a student's ability to sort out what is important and what is not. Because chronic stress can cause the brain and body to deplete available nutrients, no energy is left for learning. Stress also suppresses the growth of brain connections which results in slow thinking and lower achievement. Thus, stress can inhibit both critical and creative thinking and short and long-term memory.

The effects of chronic stress seem like a vicious cycle. Stress makes many students more susceptible to sicknesses such as stomachaches and headaches, respiratory problems, eating disorders and colds. Many high stress kids develop nervous habits or have difficulty sleeping. Test anxiety also contributes to sickness, which may mean absenteeism and missed classes which in turn contribute to lower test scores and underachievement since the student hasn't been in class to learn the material.

Some children cope better with stress than others. More resilient children seem to have the capacity to bounce back from problems and adversity. The ability to cope with stress isn't dependent on talent or intellect, but on the child's ability to believe in himself or herself, to keep going and to trust that he/she can make it. Such students tend to be problem solvers who can see alternatives in situations they are facing.

Children with easygoing, engaging temperaments and the ability to reach out to others usually do better in the face of stress. Kids who tend to do well in spite of the stresses they face typically have someone either at home or at school who makes them feel loved, competent and strong. This is a critical factor in a child's ability to cope with stress in life.

Learners with low stress levels are better able to memorize, see relationships and patterns, understand broad theories and themes, and learn a wider range of material. To encourage achievement in all students, we need to help those children who have high levels of stress and help them develop stress management skills.

A first step is to help them understand what stress is, what causes it and how to recognize their own stress level. Use the **Measuring Your Stress Level** worksheet on the next page as a beginning activity with your students. The discussion which comes from this activity and the student's own creations of stress measurement instruments can provide a beginning focus in dealing with this widespread problem.

On subsequent pages you will see a list of suggestions for helping both individual students and your whole class learn to manage the various stresses in their lives.

MEASURING YOUR STRESS LEVEL

 Use the measuring cup illustrated below to determine your level of stress. How much stress is just right for you? Are you feeling bored at the bottom or like you're overflowing off the deep end? **Mark your present stress level on the cup.**

No one stress level is right for everyone. Depending on where you are on the measuring cup, you may need to lower or raise your level of stress, either by slowing down or by adding more spark or excitement to your life. Some stress, called **eustress**, is good. It keeps you lively and alert. But too much stress, particularly bad stress or **distress**, is a killer according to medical experts. **Distress** or bad stress can be found at either level of the measuring cup. We all want to strive for the level that is JUST RIGHT.

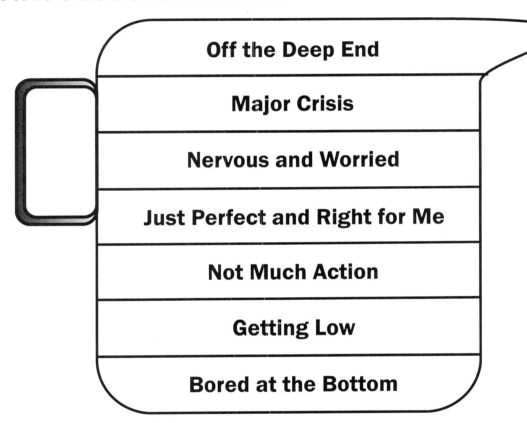

Off the Deep End

Major Crisis

Nervous and Worried

Just Perfect and Right for Me

Not Much Action

Getting Low

Bored at the Bottom

STUDENT ACTIVITIES

1. Mark your present stress level on the measuring cup.
2. Discuss: What are some ways you know you are on this level?
3. Is this a good level for you? _____ Why?
4. Draw an arrow to show whether your stress level is stable, rising, or falling.
5. Design and draw your own Stress Measurement Instrument. Indicate levels and give each level a creative but appropriate name. Mark your present stress level on your instrument. Draw an arrow in the direction you think your stress level is headed. Share with the class or a small group.

NOTES

Strategies for Helping Children Manage Stress

1. Understand each child's stress level.

Look for symptoms of stress without punishing symptomatic behavior. An awareness of high levels of stress will help you to understand each child and begin to look for ways to deal with the causes of stress.

2. Spend time listening.

Many children go days and even weeks without anyone really listening to their feelings, fears and concerns. Clear up their misconceptions as you encourage them to express their feelings appropriately. Reassure each child that you care about him/her.

3. Lessen the stress level by telling your students what to expect in the future.

The anticipation that something negative may happen is always worse than the event itself. To verify this, just remember the last time you waited in a dentist's office before getting a filling or having a root canal! Help your students navigate future unknowns by giving them as much information as you can about what is going to happen the next day, the next week, the next grading period, etc.

4. Encourage your students to be proactive problem solvers by expressing opinions, suggestions, and solutions for the future.

Teach problem solving strategies such as brainstorming, decision making, forecasting, and planning. Show how they can apply these strategies to stressful situations in their lives.

NOTES

5. Discourage perfectionism by talking about your past failures and mistakes.

Stories about the mistakes and failures of their teachers and parents fascinate kids! While you might be hesitant to share a story that makes you look foolish or inept, this could teach a valuable lesson. The message is that no one is perfect, yet everyone can still become successful and worthwhile by learning from mistakes and moving ahead. What an important lesson this is for all children.

6. Encourage the development of competence and independence.

Stressful situations will never completely disappear from life. A child who thinks all his problems and stressors will disappear when he grows up is in for a rude awakening! Children who develop an ability to be competent and independent problem solvers for the situations in their own lives will be much better able to cope with the stresses of adult life. Children who are always rescued or shielded from problems don't develop the coping strategies they will need in the future.

7. Help each child discover relaxation techniques that work for him or her.

Each of us has our own favorite ways of relaxing. Some of us like to curl up on the sofa and read while others like to jog. Some of us like to listen to classical music while others would rather dance at a nightclub. In the same way, each child will have preferred activities for relaxation. These need to be discovered, validated and used.

8. Use appropriate behavior management techniques.

Part of school stress comes from chaotic, noisy, out-of-control classrooms. Good behavior

NOTES

management brings predictability coupled with the knowledge that the teacher has a handle on everything. This is a great stress reliever for students, as it is for teachers as well!

9. Find support systems for students who lack them.

Some students have wonderful support systems consisting of a loving family and friends. These are most likely the students who manage stress well. Others have little in the way of family support or close friendships. For such students, work to find or establish support systems where they can share and talk over their problems. Some schools have established small support groups for students who have divorced parents, who have gone through an incidence of child abuse, or who seem to have no friends.

10. Use humor and laughter.

"Because of laughter along the way, one can enjoy the journey and arrive refreshed." - Source unknown

Laughter is one of life's best stress relievers! Most of us know that laughter is relaxing and makes us feel good. Recent scientific research shows that laughter actually changes the body chemistry and fills us with beneficial enzymes and hormones. A joyful classroom climate produces laughter, reduces stress and promotes learning. Make sure you and your students laugh together every day.

11. Engage in storytelling.

When our children were growing up, our family had a favorite story which had different plots and endings each time we told it. It always began, *"Once upon a time, a long, long time ago, in a deep, dark forest there lived a WHALE!"* The whale

NOTES

continually played the role of the omnipresent protector who would be there in the face of any stress or difficulty. As our children grew, the context of the story changed, as did the various stressors in their lives. Still, the whale stories remained. These stories continue from time to time even now and serve as a reminder they can manage stress and overcome adversity. What a terrific stress reliever!

12. Include assignments/lessons/questions with no right or wrong answers.

Open-ended questions are often used to teach critical and creative thinking skills. Another use for this kind of question is as a stress reliever. When there is no one right answer, many kids begin to relax, their stress levels diminish and their thinking skills improve.

13. Work on test anxiety.

Use **A Test About Tests** to pinpoint the specific cause or causes of test anxiety. This is the first step in dealing with and solving the problem. After using this simple assessment to target problem areas, brainstorm ways to deal with the specific forms of test anxiety that are present for each student.

14. Teach time management skills.

Not having enough time to do everything that needs to be done is a common stressor for both kids and adults. Many students don't have enough time because they waste much of the time they have. Ask your students to use the checklist **Typical Time Wasters for Students** to identify their major time wasters. Then help them develop a plan to stop wasting time in these areas. If they follow their plan, this will be a great way to reduce their stress level.

NOTES

15. Use drama, games, exercise and classroom celebrations as stress relievers.

Hands-on activities which touch the emotions and allow for kinesthetic expression and learning are not only terrific stress relievers, but they are also a great way to encourage student achievement and motivation. Plan learning activities of this type each day.

16. If you are a teacher, talk to parents about the concerns listed below. If you are a parent, consider the concerns in relation to your own children. Dealing with any of these issues will reduce stress for most children.

- Overloading children with activities

- Returning to a simpler family life

- Limiting TV viewing and turning it off totally one or two days a week

- Building character and spiritual/moral values in children

17. Develop a specific plan for helping one child deal with stress.

Use the form on page 109 **My Plan for Helping a Child Deal with Stress** as you formulate your plan.

A TEST ABOUT TESTS

Scoring: 4 - This describes me exactly.
3 - This describes the way I usually feel.
2 - Sometimes I feel like this.
1 - I rarely feel this way.
0 - I have never felt like this.

_____ 1. I never feel prepared when I take a test.

_____ 2. I start to feel physically nervous and stressed before a test is given.

_____ 3. I can guarantee that I will not do well on any test I take.

_____ 4. The computerized test answer sheets tend to confuse me.

_____ 5. When I come across a question that I don't know, I panic.

_____ 6. I panic when others finish a test before I do, even if it's not a timed test.

_____ 7. I have mental blocks when I am taking a test.

_____ 8. I worry that I will run out of time during a timed test.

_____ 9. I look around the room and feel that everyone else taking the test knows more than I do.

_____ 10. The word **test** makes me panic.

_____ TOTAL   **Score Interpretation:**

40-31   You suffer from major test anxiety. Stress reduction techniques, a time management plan, working to build your self-confidence, and learning a variety of study skills will help.

30-21   You have problems in test taking which are due to test anxiety. Relaxation techniques before a test and using a variety of study skills will help.

20-11   You are usually relaxed in your approach to test taking. It would be helpful to pinpoint any items above in which you scored a 3 or 4. Work to improve in these areas.

Below 11   You have no test anxiety!

Taken from _Motivating Underachievers_ by Carolyn Coil, Pieces of Learning.

TYPICAL TIME WASTERS FOR STUDENTS

✎ *Check your top 5 time wasters from the list. Then develop a plan of action to improve.*

_____1. The telephone, TV and/or Internet

_____2. People who drop by my house

_____3. School meetings

_____4. Crisis situations

_____5. Lack of goals or direction

_____6. Procrastination

_____7. No self-discipline

_____8. Everyone else's priorities; inability to say *"no"*

_____9. Unclear or inaccurate information; conflicting instructions

_____10. Personal disorganization

_____11. Attempting to do too much

_____12. Unrealistic time estimates

_____13. Losing things

_____14. Not using a checklist, calendar or assignment sheet

_____15. Lack of long-range planning

_____16. Daydreaming

_____17. Excessive socializing or hanging out with friends

_____18. Not doing things correctly the first time

_____19. Playing the *savior* role with friends

_____20. Lack of knowledge/ability/motivation to begin a task

_____21. Not having a place for things

_____22. Thinking I need do everything perfectly

_____23. Driving around; cruising

_____24. Other _____

Reproducible

My Plan for Helping a Child Deal With Stress

Name of child _____

1. Describe the situation or stressor facing the child:

2. Ways I can remove or change the source of stress for the child or if the source cannot be changed, ways I can remove or change some of the symptoms:

3. Ways I can help the child in getting away from the source of stress or in preventing it from happening:

4. Ways I can help the child learn to live with the stress:

5. My plan of action is:

**"Who dares to teach
must never cease to learn."**
**John Cotton Dana,
motto composed for
Kean College, New Jersey**

DEALING WITH THE PROBLEMS OF SOCIETY AND POP CULTURE

Dealing With the Problems of Society and Pop Culture

A gang within the class is shoplifting at a local convenience store. Peer pressure and the need to belong strengthen their membership . . . Kids hang out at the local mall or video arcade. They spend hours there but say they have no time for homework . . . The media portrays the good student as a nerd or oddball while encouraging consumer driven **nonconformist conformity** . . . The belief held by many kids is that anyone can become rich quick by doing well in sports or selling drugs.

Problems of Society

The scenarios above reflect what Jack Frymier says in his book <u>Growing Up is Risky Business</u>: *"The problems that most children face lie outside the school rather than inside, on the street rather than the playground, and in the living room rather than the classroom."*

How true this statement is! During the past 30 years, but most especially during the 1990s, the myriad of social problems that are plaguing our society as a whole flooded the schools. These problems don't stop at the schoolhouse door. They affect all aspects of school life. Some examples are:

- Vulgar and abusive language
- Teenage pregnancy
- Drug abuse
- Guns and Violence
- Child abuse and neglect
- Poverty
- Absentee fathers
- Lack of adult supervision

The social and educational effects of these problems are widespread. One major concern is that so many children are growing up in poverty. A 1991 Fordham University study shows that the number of American children living in poverty has grown steadily. The poverty rate in the United States throughout the 1990s has been approximately 25%. That means one out of every four children we try to educate in our schools is living in poverty, more than double the rate in any other industrialized nation. Another study done in 1993 by the Center for the Study of Social Policy shows that 44% of African American children and 38% of Hispanic children live in homes below the poverty level. Poverty often breeds many of the social problems listed above, but these problems can come from all parts of the economic spectrum.

At one point in our history, schools were considered successful when they taught students the basic skills. Because of the social problems occurring in so many homes and communities, we are now calling upon schools to meet even more basic needs. We must devote time in the school day to counseling and psychological services, sex and substance abuse education, parenting classes, breakfast programs and after school care. We must attend to these needs before we can begin to encourage achievement in the purely academic realm.

The Messages and Attitudes of Pop Culture and the Media

Our cultural and societal values and attitudes have changed greatly. Education is often not a priority in the home or in the culture as a whole. Many consider sports, popular culture, money, and social life to be more important than academic achievement. As a result, many students feel that nearly everything else in modern life is more important and interesting than schoolwork. They idolize sports heroes and music, fashion, film and television stars who often have more influence over their minds than parents and teachers do. All of this does little to show kids why academic achievement is important at all.

Our affluent culture often emphasizes exotic vacations, brand name clothing, and rampant consumption and materialism. A 1993 survey of employers who were interviewing high school seniors searching for their first job revealed a lack of a *work ethic* mentality among many students. Instead, they found an attitude of *society owes me* and questions such as *"What's the least amount of work I can get away with?"* These reflect a common mind set for many of our students. Instead of incorporating the work ethic where each person works hard and earns his or her way in society, many kids now feel that society owes them a comfortable lifestyle.

So many different values and activities compete for our children's time and attention! Soap operas with their manipulative characters and sexual innuendoes rule the afternoons for many kids. Pop culture heroes are jocks, rock musicians and superstars. Their message is that popularity and money are more important than brains and hard work. This seductive message is tough to counteract!

The messages of today's pop culture run contrary to the skills and values needed for achievement in school. Achievement of a long-term goal requires hard work from students; pop culture preaches instant gratification and having it all right now. Kids' attitudes toward school reflect the viewpoints of pop culture. Schoolwork does, after all, take work. Many students who do not possess a work ethic mentality need encouragement because they do not feel it is necessary to put forth any effort or to do any work.

Overall, education gets poor press. If 9,999 students go to school every day and work hard while one student goes to school and sells drugs, the media will not report about the 9,999. Yet that one student is likely to become the lead story on the 6:00 news. If 100 teachers are teaching creative, engaging lessons, and one teacher abuses a student, the abusive teacher will make the headlines, not the 100 teachers who are doing a good job! The one student or one teacher who is doing something wrong gets all of the attention. Unfortunately, when the media reports a story, which in reality is an isolated incident, people generalize it to include all teachers, all students or all schools.

Our society gives lip service to the importance of education but does not give it much financial or emotional support. Society expects schools to be the miracle workers for all problems and for the ills of society - to do it with little money and lots of criticism. This is a difficult task to say the least!

Many educators feel discouraged because of these major problems and societal attitudes. Changing society seems like an impossible task. While we may be unable to change society as a whole, we should not give up or say the situation is impossible. We can use several strategies to encourage achievement as we deal with the problems and concerns discussed in this chapter.

Strategies to Encourage Achievement

NOTES

1. Contact and collaborate with local radio and TV broadcasters and newspaper reporters.

Set up a meeting with the news policy makers in your area. With them, help establish a policy that part of each newscast or newspaper will highlight academics and the achievements of students in local schools. The local media tends to be responsive to the needs and concerns of the people they serve. Local media outlets act upon proactive, practical suggestions and plans, especially when they come from a group such as the PTA, student council or booster club. Over time, a new, more positive reporting policy could have a major impact.

2. Model the work ethic mentality and send the message that every job is a job worth doing well.

Parts of every job are tedious and boring or can be done in a minimal way, including portions of the job of teaching. Discuss these with your students and demonstrate your dedication to a work ethic by doing your tedious tasks well.

3. Show real life examples of workers with and those without an education.

As part of a school-to-work project or a study of careers, help your students see differences in the types of work done by people who have less than a high school education, those who are high school graduates and those who have a college degree. Display findings and conclusions on charts, dia-

NOTES

grams, graphs. Discuss why education is important, using these real life examples.

4. Organize extracurricular activities within the school that encourage positive friendships.

One reason kids get into trouble after school is that they have no worthwhile activities to fill their afternoon hours. This problem is most prevalent with middle and high school students who are too old for child care and too young for jobs. A percentage of these students are already involved in outside activities organized by their parents, but the rest have empty hours to fill. These are the kids who do not naturally join in and need special encouragement to participate in extracurricular activities. The special encouragement and interest of a teacher may be just the thing to get them involved in a positive activity.

5. Meet with parents and talk about ways to monitor out-of-school activities.

Parents do not want their children to wander aimlessly after school, nor do they want them hanging out on a local street corner or at the mall. Yet many parents feel they have no control over their children's activities and do not have the skills to monitor their kids. Most parents are very interested in practical suggestions to solve this problem. Organize an evening parent meeting to brainstorm ideas and formulate plans of action to deal with this problem.

6. Increase your emphasis on character development, community building, positive school climate, and social/emotional skills.

Many schools have adopted formal character education or social skills programs, while others

use a less structured approach. The important thing is to plan specific ways to develop your students' intra personal and interpersonal skills. These skills do not develop automatically for most children but are extremely necessary to become a well-functioning member of society.

7. Develop micro societies within the classroom or grade level which simulate society in real life.

These micro societies can be a miniature town with a bank, post office, a store, etc. They can also be simulations which involve budget planning, child care, home buying, and other **real life** activities. Micro societies help students learn in a concrete way that life is not always as glamorous or easy as it appears on TV shows and in the movies.

8. Select students to shadow adults through the workday.

Choose a variety of occupations and careers and have students share what they have learned with the rest of the class. Students as young as 3rd or 4th grade can do this activity. It is always high interest and provides students with a realistic look at the world outside school.

9. Recommend that high school students work at a job no more than 20 hours a week.

A recent report by the National Research Council shows that many high school students find themselves in a vicious cycle. They work to buy a car which, in turn, they need as transportation to get to work which, in turn, they must go to - in order to pay for the car! Some high school students work 35 hours a week or more. This discourages achievement because there is no time for home-

NOTES

work or study, no time for extracurricular activities and no time for friendships. Often these students are so tired they sleep in class. Some work experience encourages achievement, but more than 20 hours a week tends to have the opposite effect.

10. Capitalize on your students' interest in sports by using sports analogies to help them understand the concepts of goal setting, long-range planning, effort and persistence.

Use the reproducible worksheet on the next page relating these ideas to success and achievement in school and at home.

11. Discuss social problems in your area with a group of colleagues or at a faculty meeting.

Brainstorm possible solutions using the *Teacher Reflection Page: Societal Problems* to guide your discussion.

What Can You Learn from the World of Sports?

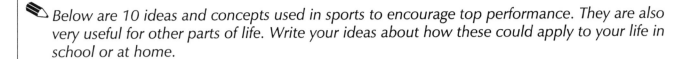

✎ *Below are 10 ideas and concepts used in sports to encourage top performance. They are also very useful for other parts of life. Write your ideas about how these could apply to your life in school or at home.*

1. Show up for practice and for the main event.

2. Know where you're heading and know what the goal is.

3. Have several game plans, not just one.

4. Don't count on the one thing that is the least likely to occur.

5. Work toward small goals (short-term goals) to reach larger goals.

6. Practice skills before the big performance.

7. Don't give up because you get a penalty or make a mistake.

8. Figure out what you want to accomplish and then plan backwards.

9. Have a coach and have people who cheer you on.

10. Work as a team to get things done.

TEACHER REFLECTION PAGE
SOCIETAL PROBLEMS

A List of Typical Problems in Urban, Suburban and Rural Areas

Urban
1. Drugs
2. Alcohol widely available
3. Poverty
4. Single parent homes
5. Parents working 2 or 3 jobs - kids are raising other kids
6. Parents blame school for the problem, not the child
7. Fear of violence and crime - violence is an everyday happening
8. Children 'hanging out' late at night

9. Other:

Suburban
1. Drugs
2. Alcoholism (more hidden)
3. Corporate downsizing and mergers
4. Single parent homes
5. Absentee parents - sitters raising children (Home Alone syndrome)
6. Parents blame school or a teacher for the problem, not the child
7. Fear of crime, mostly from what is reported by the media
8. Kids are working to buy cars, clothes, and other items

9. Other:

Rural
1. Education not a priority
2. Limited job market/opportunities
3. Lack of constructive social activities
4. Minimum exposure to culture or enrichment
5. "Good Ol' Boy" network powerful in school boards
6. Resistance to change
7. Dysfunction, alcohol, drugs
8. Limited accelerated/advanced/honors classes because of smaller population
9. Other:

For Discussion and Reflection:

Which problems do you see as most prevalent in your area?

What are some strategies you can use to encourage achievement in students living with these problems?

Reproducible

TV and Video Games:
How Much is Too Much?

"Turn off the TV and go outside and play," an exasperated mother said to her two sons aged 8 and 10. *"There's nothing to do!"* they replied as they reluctantly turned off the cartoon show they were watching. A half hour later they were back in the house with the TV on again. *"It's just easier to let them watch it,"* their mother reluctantly decided.

Situations like the one described above are commonplace in American homes. Ninety-nine percent of all households in America have at least one TV. Americans watch an unbelievable 250 billion hours of television annually. TV has become so pervasive that turning it on is something people do reflexively when they walk into their homes or into a hotel room. We often think of the TV as background noise, yet it is designed to capture our attention and entertain us while we *veg out*. It flashes visual stimuli which can be instantly replayed. Because of television, children have come to regard amusement and being entertained as their right and boredom or work as an infringement on that right.

Additionally, new brain research tells us that children need a variety of stimulating inputs and a flood of information. However, this should not come from television. Television is two-dimensional while the brain needs depth and three-dimensional learning. Furthermore, television with its fast visual pace allows no time for reflection or interaction. It allows no time for the eyes to relax or to integrate the information. Many neuroscientists and experts in brain development say they would ban television entirely for children under the age of eight.

Kids are enthusiastic consumers of the themes portrayed by television. These tend to have an excess of fame, fortune, aggression, and sexuality without much thoughtful reflection to put them in perspective. Children often reenact what they see on TV. For many years educators have voiced concern about the potential negative effects of television violence and sex.

Television producers have begun a voluntary program rating system, though its effectiveness has not as yet been proven. While these ratings are minimally helpful, most parents need more guidance than ratings can possibly provide. Instead of assuming any show with a certain rating is good for children to watch, why not develop guidelines for good television watching one hour a day? This way parents could pick the best programs and send the message that an hour of TV per day is enough for any child!

According to a study by the United States Department of Education, excessive television watching is one reason for low scores on 8th grade achievement tests. Another study found that the more television children watch, the lower their reading scores will be. It is reasonable to assume that students who spend a large portion of their after school hours watching television will spend a smaller amount of time doing homework and studying.

Though they are interactive, video games pose many of the same problems in terms of a child's development. The visual stimuli are still two-dimensional and the violence in many video games has the potential to affect children in negative ways. As with TV watching, a small amount of time playing video games is all that is needed.

Secretary of Education Richard W. Riley recommends that parents limit their children's television viewing. Academic achievement drops sharply for children who watch more than 10 hours of TV during the school week. Instead, children should spend part of their free time each day working on a project or area of interest, playing a game, reading, or even daydreaming. These activities are beneficial only when they are away from the television.

Playing outside games such as hopscotch, kickball, "Simon Says," and other loosely organized childhood games are much more helpful to children than watching TV during the same time period.

One of the harshest critics of the negative effects of television on children is Attorney General Janet Reno. Perhaps one reason for this is that her parents encouraged her achievement and interests both inside and outside the classroom by never owning a television. The Reno children lived on a rural homestead and instead of watching television their parents urged them to play games, explore, build things, and learn about the natural environment. Janet Reno's mother claimed watching TV would give her children **mind rot**. She may have been right!

Like the Reno family a generation ago, in 1995 the Ashcraft family of Orlando, Florida, decided to unplug their TV and not watch it anymore. "Absence," says Michael Ashcraft, "does make the heart grow fonder, not of TV but of going without it." He reports newly found interests in reading a book, talking to your family and discovering what is in one's own backyard. His children enjoy playing outdoors in their tree house and using their trampoline. They also like to do puzzles, make up songs and plays, and play card and board games.

Teachers do not have direct control over how much TV their students watch. Parents have more control, though children left in childcare situations, with babysitters or visiting friends and relatives, may end up watching more TV than parents would want.

Some first steps in learning to control television viewing and its effects are on the next page. Share these guidelines with parents and other care-givers.

Facts and Guidelines About Television Viewing

Some Facts About TV and Your Child:

- Watching television may encourage your child to think that being constantly entertained is his or her right and entitlement.

- Excessive TV watching leaves little time for homework, studying or creative thinking.

- The fast pace of television's visual images leaves no time for your child's eyes to relax or to integrate information into the brain.

- Children who watch lots of TV often have trouble paying attention to things that are not as fast paced and visual, such as school textbooks.

- Academic achievement drops sharply for children who spend more than 10 hours a week watching TV.

- Children may reenact the violence, sexuality, bad or vulgar language and disrespect they see on TV.

- Ads on TV encourage children to want things they would never think about without suggestive advertising. Many products pitched to kids on TV are not good for them!

Guidelines:

- At the beginning of the week, help your children pick one program per day they want to watch. Watch this program with them and discuss it together afterwards.

- Limit television viewing to a total of 10 hours a week or less.

- Have at least one day a week in your home when no one turns on the TV at all.

- With your children, brainstorm ideas for activities they would like to do instead of watching TV. Keep an ongoing list of these activities on the refrigerator or in another prominent place.

- Encourage reading in your home. Limit your own TV viewing and read a good book instead. Have your children follow up on an interesting TV program by finding a book in the library on the same topic or theme.

- Speak out about commercials or programs which show violence, taking a pill, or coming up with easy but unrealistic answers as solutions to complex problems.

"The test and the use of man's education
is that he finds pleasure
in the exercise of his mind."

Jacques Barzun, in Saturday Evening Post

INDEPENDENT LEARNING ACTIVITIES

Independent Learning Activities

> Mr. Clark had recently attended a professional development workshop at which the presenter emphasized the need for students to become independent, autonomous learners. In a workshop discussion group, he and several other teachers agreed that this was important, but they didn't see their middle school students developing in this way. In fact, most of the time their students had to be watched every minute even to get the minimal work done. Mr. Clark needed some specific, practical suggestions for encouraging students' independent learning.

Independent Learning

Because knowledge is increasing so rapidly and because our students must continue to learn long after they leave our classrooms, it is essential they develop skills in independent learning. Gifted and other high ability students in particular often need to engage in independent learning activities when they compact out of regular classroom assignments. Like Mr. Clark, most teachers see the need for independent learning, but encouraging students to take the responsibility for doing this seems like a daunting task.

This chapter includes two important and successful strategies for guiding and encouraging our students as they begin to learn independently. These are **Learning Centers** and **Independent Study**.

Both strategies have been around for a long time and are familiar to many teachers. Unfortunately, some teachers have had negative experiences when they used them. If this is the case with you, don't let past experiences discourage you! The keys to success with both strategies are found in careful planning, good preparation, and setting specific behavioral and work requirements for students.

Learning Centers

Look at the guidelines for learning centers and at the graphic organizers for planning found on the next pages. Try the format that suits you best. Three specialized learning centers, the **Question Box Learning Center,** the **Blockbuster Movie Review Center,** and the **Clean Out Your File Cabinet Learning Center,** are also included. Each of these is highly motivational for students, is self-perpetuating and you can use them all year.

Establishing a learning center is a good way to start to encourage your students to work independently.

Using Learning Centers to Encourage Achievement

General Guidelines

Consider the following as you plan your learning center.

Logistics

- Must be structured so that the child can work independently with a minimum of direct instruction by the teacher.

- May be structured or used as an alternate activity when a student is doing curriculum compacting or when the student works at a faster pace than other students.

- Must fit into available physical space within your classroom or school.

- Should be feasible given the resources of the school, grade level or classroom.

- Should utilize available supplies, materials and technologies.

- Can be displayed on a backboard, poster or bulletin board, or can be in a container of some type.

- Should be visually attractive. Packaging is important!

- Must have a system for storing the students' partially finished work.

Content

- Should provide opportunities for higher level thinking and in-depth learning.

- May be based on a specific theme or topic or may be generic and guide the student in studying his/her topic of interest.

- May be done chronologically featuring activities appropriate for each day, week or season of the year.

- May feature various types of questions.

- Should have many activities for students to choose from based on several different learning styles or modalities, multiple intelligences or the various levels of Bloom's taxonomy.

- Should state specific criteria for assessment and may include student self-assessment, peer assessment and teacher assessment.

- Should include activities which can be done individually and activities which can be done in partners, trios and/or groups of four. More than this makes too many students working on one activity!

Planning a Learning Center

Theme or Topic _____

Student Activity	Product	Materials Needed

Reproducible

Plan for Learning Center Activities

Topic: _____

Visual Activities
List activities and materials below:

Kinesthetic Activities
List activities and materials below:

Technological Activities
List activities and materials below:

Auditory/Verbal Activities
List activities and materials below:

Question Box Learning Center

The purpose of this learning center is to help students in generating and answering their own questions. Because the students generate the questions, this center can become a self-perpetuating learning activity to use throughout the school year. Some type of display and a place for storing the various forms is all that teachers need to make this a successful learning activity.

Students who go to the center can:

1. Write a question when they don't know the answer. (Form 1)

2. Research their own question or another student's question and find the answer. (Form 2)

3. Research their own question or another student's question without finding the answer. (Form 3)

At the end of the week, unit of study or at other specific intervals, review the answers and discuss and research further any unsolved questions.

FORM 1

My question is _____

_____?

My name is _____

FORM 2

The question is _____

_____

_____?

The answer is _____

_____

_____

Resources I used to find the answer are:

1._____

2._____

3._____

My name is _____

Reproducible

FORM 3

The question is _____

_____?

Student 1

Resources I have tried are

1. _____

2. _____

3. _____

I have tried three resources and cannot find the answer. Can someone else find it?

My name is _____

****

Student 2

Resources I have tried are

1. _____

2. _____

3. _____

I have tried three more resources and cannot find the answer. Can someone else find it?

My name is _____

****

Student 3

Resources I have tried are

1. _____

2. _____

3. _____

I have tried 3 more resources and cannot find the answer. Help!

My name is _____

When three students have used a total of at least nine different resources and cannot find the answer, the three of you must brainstorm other possible strategies for finding the answer. Then take your list of strategies and this form to your teacher.

Blockbuster Movie Review Learning Center

Teacher Preparation:

1. Decorate a shoe box or other medium sized box with bright paper, frames or rolls of exposed film, newspaper movie review clippings or anything else with a movie theme which will capture your students' imagination.
2. Put a slit in the top of the box big enough for a 4 x 6 index card.
3. Prepare 4 x 6 cards with the following information on them:

Blockbuster Movie Review by _____

Name of movie _____

Setting:

Theme:

Archetypal elements in characters:
   (**Villain, sweet young girl, macho male, modern hero**)

Plot, conflict and crisis:

✎ *On the back of this card, write your evaluation and critique of this movie.*

---

4. Have these cards readily available for your students to use. Put completed cards in the decorated box. Other students can take them out of the box and read them, display them on a bulletin board, or share in another way. They are a great way to teach literary analysis through a source all kids are familiar with.

5. You may change the information required on the card to suit the grade and ability levels of your students. A variation on this activity is to use similar cards for reviews of TV shows or books.

This learning center is self-perpetuating and can continue as long as students are interested in doing it.

The "Clean Out Your File Cabinet" Learning Center

Most teachers have many worthwhile and enriching student activities they would like to do with their students but never have the time to get to them during the school day. Over the years, some of these activities get filed away in the file cabinet. Others can be found in supplemental activity books which end up on a bookshelf or in a storage cabinet.

One way to productively use these resources (and to clean out your files, cabinets or bookshelves at the same time) is to establish a *Choose Your Own Activity Learning Center*. Students begin using this center by establishing their own criteria for a good independent learning activity. The second step is for each student to evaluate some activity pages or books in your file cabinet or storage shelves according to these criteria. Not only does this give students choices in their learning, it also teaches them valuable lessons about evaluating and decision making, the highest level of Bloom's Taxonomy.

An evaluation form with sample criteria is below.

Rating Scale for _____ Learning Activity						
Criteria	**Scale**	**1**	**2**	**3**	**4**	**5**
Interesting to me						
Can do it independently without teacher help						
I'll learn something new						
Contains up-to-date information						
I have the materials needed to do the activity						
Total points for this activity _____						

Need a 20 or higher to use.

Your students could choose their first activity using the criteria on the above grid. However, to get the most benefit from this learning center, eventually they need to learn to develop their own criteria because this teaches an important higher level thinking skill.

Independent Study

> *"We have a whole week of independent study,"* Kyle confided to his best friend Josh. *"That means we can go to the media center and fool around on the Internet all week. I'll show you some cool race car sites I found on my home computer. Don't worry about the assignment. We'll just tell Ms. Taylor we didn't have time to finish it."*
>
> *"Independent study,"* thought Maureen. *"I want to get an 'A' on my report. The easiest way to do that is to just copy parts of the encyclopedia, cut and paste some things from the computer, change a few words and make a nice cover. I don't think the teacher actually reads the reports anyway. I just need to make it look and sound good."*
>
> *Topic too broad* → *"The teacher said we could choose our own independent study topic,"* Ramon told his mother. *"I think I'll do a study about Space. I know I can find lots of information on that topic!"*
>
> *Topic too narrow* → Caitlin worked and worked on her independent study project. She had chosen to study women's fashions in 18th century Virginia because she was interested in fashion and clothes. The problem was that she couldn't find very much information on her topic, and her report and illustrations did not really reflect all of the time she had spent searching for information in vain. The night before her independent study project was due, she was almost in tears. *"This is a horrible project, yet I've worked so hard!"* she thought to herself.

The students scenarios above exemplify typical problems that occur when students do independent study.

- Like Kyle, some students see independent study as an opportunity to fool around, goof off and surf the Net. These students really don't study very much while doing independent study.

- Others are conscientious like Maureen but lack confidence in their own abilities. They become dependent on one source which they feel will give the correct information and make them look good.

- Ramon exemplifies students who choose a topic which is much too broad. These students have so much information to sift through they find it hard to focus, decide what is important and do a thorough job.

• Caitlin has the opposite problem. Her topic is too narrow to study well with the sources and information that are available to her. She has worked hard but has become very discouraged.

Besides the problems exemplified by these students, there is also a problem with reliability of sources. When most sources were in print from reputable publishers, reliability was not as much of a problem. However, with the arrival of Internet sources and self-publishing, all of this has changed. We must teach students to discriminate and recognize reliable and less reliable sources.

Several resources are included on the following pages of this book. They are designed to help teachers and students deal with some of the problems discussed above. Use them for your students and your learning objectives and outcomes.

• Two mindmaps show a variety of **Activities** your students can do as they pursue an independent study and a potpourri of ideas for **Products** they can create. These give a number of different options and approaches for independent study. Before the student begins his or her research specific activities and products should be chosen by the student and/or the teacher.

• Use the **Independent Study Action Guide** as a broad guideline for students to choose and narrow their topics of study and for directing how many and what types of sources they will use.

• The **Print and Internet Sources Record Sheets** provide a way for students to record each of their sources along with pertinent information about credentials, where the source can be found, etc. This also helps with reliability.

• Several pages of guidelines for **Reliability of Sources** (print, e-mail and web sources) are included. There is a simpler version for primary students and a more complex version for older students. You may want to use these guidelines as the basis for a separate unit of study about reliability.

• Use the pages when you want to develop skills in recognizing different types of sources, ideas and information. These forms are particularly useful in developing the higher level thinking skills of analysis, synthesis and evaluation.

Activities

Color in blue activities you like to do. Color in green 6 activities you would like to try.

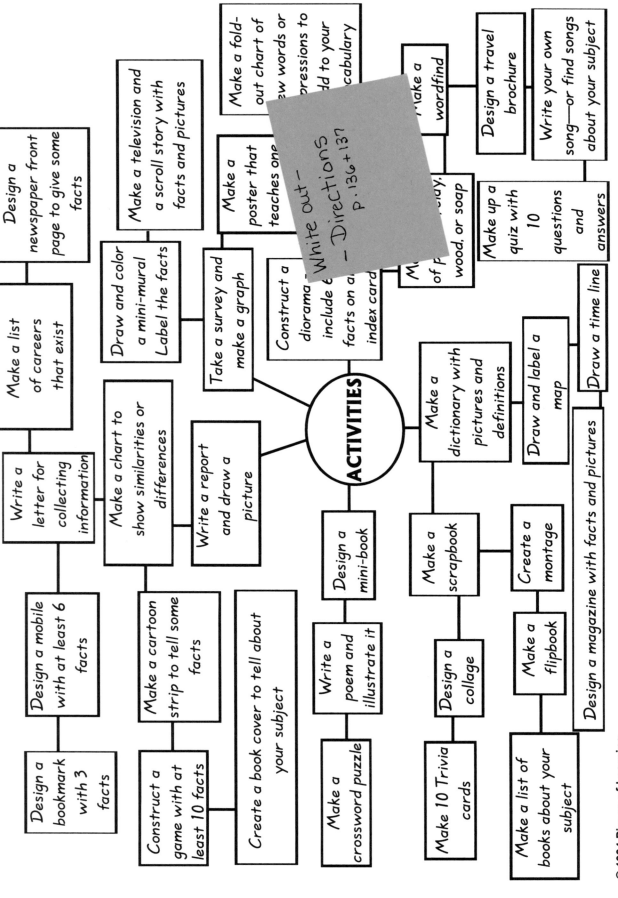

Design a newspaper front page to give some facts

Make a list of careers that exist

Write a letter for collecting information

Design a mobile with at least 6 facts

Design a bookmark with 3 facts

Make a television and a scroll story with facts and pictures

Draw and color a mini-mural. Label the facts

Make a chart to show similarities or differences

Make a cartoon strip to tell some facts

Construct a game with at least 10 facts

Make a fold out chart of new words or expressions to add to your vocabulary

Make a poster that teaches one

Take a survey and make a graph

Construct a diorama - include facts on an index card

Write a report and draw a picture

Create a book cover to tell about your subject

White out – Directions – p. 136+137

Make a wordfind

Design a travel brochure

Write your own song—or find songs about your subject

Make up a quiz with 10 questions and answers

ACTIVITIES

Make a dictionary with pictures and definitions

Draw and label a map

Draw a time line

Design a magazine with facts and pictures

Design a mini-book

Make a scrapbook

Create a montage

Write a poem and illustrate it

Design a collage

Make a flipbook

Make a crossword puzzle

Make 10 Trivia cards

Make a list of books about your subject

from *Thematic Activities for Student Portfolios*

Products

Color in blue products you like to produce. Color in green 6 products you would like to try.

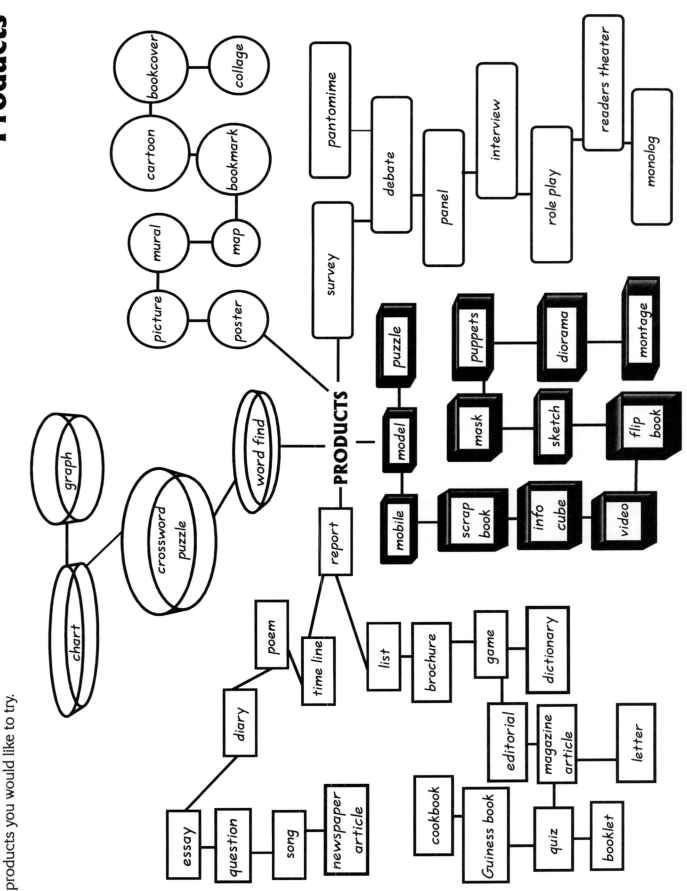

from *Thematic Activities for Student Portfolios*

Independent Study Action Guide

Broad topic of interest: _____

✏️ *1. With a partner, brainstorm subtopics. Most of the time a broad topic could have as many as 50-100 subtopics! Write all the subtopics you can think of on a separate sheet of paper.*

✏️ *2. Go to the school library or media center for 45 minutes or less. Choose several subtopics that particularly interest you and find out if there is information available about them. Choose four subtopics that interest you and that you can get information about. Write them in the spaces below.*

_____   _____

_____   _____

✏️ *3. Pick one of the four subtopics for your independent study. Circle it.*

Using Secondary Sources

- Secondary sources are not original sources. They contain information about your topic from the point of view of someone who has done research on the topic and has learned about it.

- Secondary sources can be books, magazines, newspapers, videos, tapes, information from the Internet, etc.

- Some secondary sources are more reliable than others. That is, some sources are considered more believable or trustworthy than others. Less reliable sources may be those that are out-of-date or some unedited sources on the Internet. Use reliable secondary sources. (See guidelines.)

- Record each secondary source you use on the forms found on the following pages. As you take notes, make sure you know which source your information comes from.

- Use at least _____ secondary sources in this independent study. At least half must be print sources. The rest may be from software, audio-visual sources, multimedia resources or the Internet.

Using Primary Sources

- Primary sources are firsthand or original sources of information. An eyewitness account, an interview you conduct with someone who did research or an experiment, or your own observations and conclusions are types of primary sources.

- Another way to obtain information through a primary source is to conduct an experiment or survey yourself. Be sure to keep accurate observations and data so you are a reliable primary source!

- Use at least _____ primary sources in this independent study.

Print Sources Record Sheet

Call Number or Other Locator	Author or Title	Publisher and Date	Pages used	Location and Other Information

Internet Sources Record Sheet

E-mail address Or Website	Author, Organization, Title	Date written, revised or visited	Person's or Organization's Credentials	Contact information (other than the Internet)

Reliability of Sources - General Guidelines

Using good search tools, critical thinking skills and appropriate research strategies are the keys to finding valuable information. Consult trained media specialists and librarians who have excellent information management skills concerning which sources are reliable.

Judging how _reliable_ the sources of information are that you use in your research is difficult. Use the questions on the next pages as guidelines for determining the reliability of your sources. The forms show a method for evaluating ideas and information and for evaluating and classifying sources.

Print sources

- What is the copyright date? Is this an updated version of an older book or article? The date something was written could affect its accuracy. Many sources become outdated quickly.

- Can you find two sources that say the same thing or give you the same information? If so, this indicates both sources are probably reliable.

- Is the source a respected source in the profession or area you are researching?

- Can you verify the facts presented by asking a knowledgeable person in this field of study?

- Who is the publisher? What is the publisher's reputation? Did the author pay to have the work printed? Check with a librarian or your school media specialist to help you answer these questions.

- Is the point of view opinionated or slanted in a particular way? If so, this may not be a reliable source.

- If your source is a newspaper or magazine, is the article an editorial/opinion column or a report of the facts?

- If your source cites surveys, polls or studies, were these funded by a person or group who wants you to see things from their point of view?

- Does the author or publisher have a political agenda or a hidden agenda? In other words, do they have a special reason for wanting you to believe the facts the way they have presented them?

- If your source is in a magazine or newspaper, is it an advertisement? You can tell if it is because this will be noted in small print somewhere on the page. An advertisement may have some good information in it, but it will usually present a slanted point of view rather than an unbiased point of view.

E-mail sources

- Consider the e-mail address itself. Is it connected with an institution? Some indicators are an address ending in edu (educational institution), gov (government), org (organization) or mil (military). Net and com indicate commercial services.

- What country, if any is indicated? Be aware that people can purchase e-mail or web addresses from other countries, so this is not always a good indicator.

- Is the e-mail address linked to a web page?

- Will the person give you a postal address, phone or fax number?

- Will your source tell you his or her place of business?

- Can you verify the street address or place of business using a search engine?

- Will they give you the name of another person who can corroborate what they are saying?

- Can the person give you the names of some published print sources you could find which say the same thing he/she is saying?

- What are the person's qualifications and credentials?

Web sources

- Can you find two different web sites that are not linked yet say the same thing or give you the same information? If so, this indicates both sources are probably reliable.

- Is the web page developed by a respected source in the profession or area you are researching?

- Can you find the name of the organization sponsoring the web site by using a search engine? What are other people saying about this organization?

- Do all of the hypertext links cited on the web page take you to internal pages on the same site? This may indicate a slanted point of view. If the links are to external sources, are these reliable?

- Does the point of view seem opinionated or slanted in a particular way? What biases may the author have?

- Can you verify the facts presented through another source?

- Does the web page have a bibliography? If so, does it include books and other print resources and technological resources?

- If surveys, polls or studies are cited, were these funded by a person or group who wants you to see things from their point of view?

- What are the credentials or background of the organization or person sponsoring this web site?

- Is there a way to e-mail or contact that person or organization?

- When was the site created? When was it last revised? How many hits has it gotten? A site with many hits is probably a reliable source.

Reliability of Sources
General Guidelines for Primary Students

Sometimes it is hard to know whether something you read or hear or see is true or not. Thinking about the questions below will help you decide if you have a good source of information.

Books, Magazines and Newspapers

1. What is the copyright date or the date it was printed? Is it too old to be factual? This will depend on what you are studying. If you are researching something that needs new information, you should look for a recent date.

2. Can you find two different books, magazines or newspapers that say the same thing?

3. Is the author or publisher well known? Ask your teacher or media specialist.

4. Is the information based on facts or does it seem to be someone's opinion?

5. If your source is from a newspaper or magazine, is it an opinion column? Is it advertising a product? Is it a news story?

6. Does your teacher, media specialist or parent think the information seems to be correct?

E-mail

1. What can you learn from the ending of the address? Is it edu (education), mil (military), org (organization), gov (government)? Net and com mean these are commercial online services. Other endings may mean it comes from another country.

2. Will the person sending you e-mail give you a business address, fax or phone number?

3. What is the person's background? Is he or she an expert on the topic?

4. Can you find the same or similar information in a book?

5. Will the person tell you where he or she works?

World Wide Web

1. Can you find two different web sites that say the same thing?

2. Is the person or group that wrote the web site well known? What is their background?

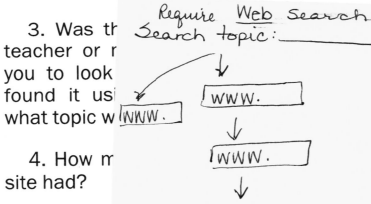

3. Was th teacher or r you to look found it usi what topic w

4. How m site had?

5. When ated? When ?

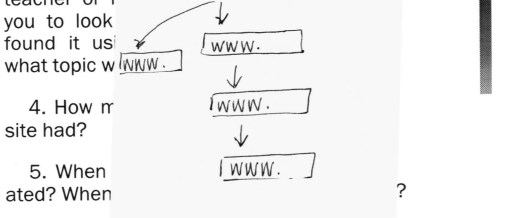

6. Does it use facts rather than opinions? Does it seem to be trying to make you believe things that don't seem to be true?

7. Does it give an e-mail address or other way to contact the person or group who developed the web site?

8. Can you find the same or similar information in books or magazines?

Evaluate and Classify Your Sources

Respected/Historically Reliable Sources	Generally respected recent sources	Questionable Sources

Evaluate and Classify Ideas and Information

Historically respected and accepted ideas, information and facts	Recent ideas still being researched and revised by experts	Off the wall controversial ideas and information

Reproducible

**"The desire of knowledge,
like the thirst of riches,
increases ever with the acquisition of it."**
Laurence Sterne, <u>Tristram Shandy</u>

CREATIVE LESSON PLANNING

Creative Lesson Planning

> It was Sunday evening. Ms. Lopez knew she had a full week ahead at school and wanted to think creatively as she planned the week's lessons. But it seemed she could think of nothing but the same old lesson plans. *"How can I encourage my students to achieve,"* she thought, *"when I don't seem to have a motivating or creative idea in my head?"*

Many teachers feel like Ms. Lopez from time to time. They want to do their best and develop inspiring, appropriate, motivating and creative lessons. Yet the ideas will just not come. At times like this, having a structure for planning creative lessons is a godsend!

This chapter shows two such structures for lesson planning. Each of these has a particular framework and pattern which make them easy to write, plan and implement.

Encounter Lessons stimulate creativity and thinking skills and are particularly useful to motivate and encourage students when starting a new unit of study. Encounter lessons begin by putting students in groups and asking them to pretend they are a specific object, person, or place. The students take turns answering a series of questions while staying in this given role. Each question relates to a specific category of response. The Extenders in Encounter Lessons comprise the unit of study for the students.

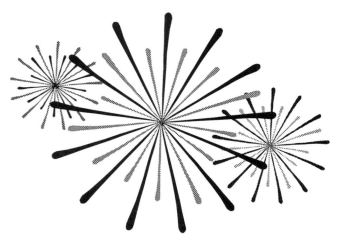

Use **Tiered Lessons** with mixed ability classes. They provide varied levels of activities that focus on key concepts or objectives. Tiered lessons encourage achievement because the levels of activities promote success for all students without being too easy and boring or too difficult and anxiety producing. In writing tiered assignments, teachers must make sure that all levels of assignments are engaging and interesting. Nothing discourages achievement faster than students thinking the other group is the one with the fun, interesting or enjoyable activity while the one they have been assigned is not.

The remaining pages in this chapter show you how to write these lessons, give sample lesson plans, and provide reproducible forms for you to use in writing your own.

Instructions for Writing and Using Encounter Lessons

Excluding the extenders, these lessons usually last from 20-30 minutes and are best done in small groups of 8-10 students. However, they also can be done in a large group setting. Encounter lessons have open-ended questions that ask the student to pretend he or she is an object and to respond accordingly. Each student responds to each question. Appoint a facilitator for each group to keep the activity focused and moving along.

Title: The title should reflect the major theme or focus of the lesson.

Boundary Breaker

This is an easily answered nonthreatening question which usually reveals something about each student's feelings or opinions. If a student does not want to answer a Boundary Breaker, he or she can say *"pass."* After everyone else has answered, the group facilitator will return to anyone who has said *"pass"* to see if they would now like to answer. If they still do not want to give an answer, they say *"pass, pass."*

Setting the Stage

This sets the scene for the questions. The group facilitator sets the stage, telling the group what person, place or object each person needs to pretend to be.

Leading Questions

1. This is the description question. In answering this question, each person should describe something.
2. This question asks for a reason and usually begins with the word *Why.*
3. This is the storytelling question. In answering this question, each person should tell a story or relate an imaginary incident that has happened.
4. This is the motto, slogan or message question. The answer to this question should be short — usually 10 words or less. Sometimes students make posters or bumper stickers with the answers to this question on them.
5. The answer to the fifth question shows some kind of change or transformation. It may be phrased as a *"What would happen if?"* question, an *"Imagine"* question, or a question that reflects a new point of view.

Extenders

The extenders are the activities in the unit of work itself. There is no limit to the number of extenders an Encounter Lesson may have. Sometimes these are student choice activities and other times they are required for everyone. The extenders could take anywhere from one or two days to several weeks to complete, depending upon how many each student has to do and how extensive they are.

Sample Encounter Lesson

Title: Famous Authors

Boundary Breaker: Tell about the best book you ever read.

Setting the Stage:

You are a famous author. You have written many books in your life. You are now quite old but would still like to write another book.

Leading Questions:

1. What type of author are you? Describe the first book you ever wrote.
Describe the types of books you usually enjoy writing.

2. Why do you think people enjoy reading your books?

3. Tell about a favorite letter you received from someone who has read your books.

4. What would you like to tell new authors who are writing their first books?

5. What new topic could you write about in your next book?

Extenders:

1. Write a letter to your favorite author. Ask interesting questions that you think he or she will respond to.

2. Write a book review of your favorite book. Put it on audio tape to make it a radio book review.

3. Make stick puppets from one of your favorite books. With a classmate, present a puppet show of a scene from the book.

4. Develop a bibliography of books written by your favorite author listed in chronological order by copyright date.

5. Design a poster advertising books by your favorite author.

6. Read a fiction book that is different from the type of book you usually read. Dress as a character from this book and tell about who you are.

7. Create a time line showing major events in your favorite book or major events in the life of your favorite author.

ENCOUNTER LESSON PLANNING FORM

Title:

Boundary Breaker:

Setting the Stage:

Leading Questions:

1. _____

2. _____

3. _____

4. _____

5. _____

Extenders:

1. _____

2. _____

3. _____

4. _____

5. _____

6. _____

SAMPLE TIERED LESSON/UNIT PLAN (Grades 4-8)

Unit/Subject/Theme: Cultural Diversity in America
Objectives:

1. To develop basic knowledge about several different cultural and ethnic groups in the United States.
2. To identify individual customs, places of origin, similarities and differences between cultural and ethnic groups.

Whole Class Activities	Assessment
1. Make a class family tree showing cultural origins of class members	1. Includes all students 2. Visually integrated
2. Read a book which is set in another culture or is about a person from another culture	1. Well organized written report 2. Includes insights about the culture

Level 1 Activity	Assessment
Make a list of holidays from various cultural groups. Draw a picture illustrating one holiday.	1. At least 6 holidays 2. Includes 3 different groups 3. Illustration shows holiday celebration clearly

Level 2 Activity	Assessment
Make a large world map labeling the ethnic/cultural origins of each person in your class.	1. Visually clear map 2. Correctly labeled 3. Includes everyone

Level 3 Activity	Assessment
Make a chart comparing and contrasting at least 3 cultures represented by students in your class.	1. Similarities and differences clearly shown 2. Accuracy of comparisons 3. Lack of stereotyping

Whole Class Culminating Activities	Assessment
1. Display illustrations, maps and charts throughout the classroom. Have one or two representatives from each level orally summarize work.	1. Each level represented 2. Clear and understandable oral presentations
2. Each student will write a journal entry reflecting on what has been learned about other cultures.	1. Clearly written 2. States new insights

Reproducible

SAMPLE TIERED LESSON/UNIT PLAN (Grades K-3)

Unit/Subject/Theme: The Planets

Objectives:

1. To learn facts and concepts about the solar system
2. To develop creativity and higher level thinking skills
3. To develop social and interpersonal skills

Whole Class Activities
1. Read or view the video of the <u>Magic School Bus Lost in the Solar System</u>.

2. Participate in solar system simulation *Orbit Around the Sun.* (See next page.)

Assessment
1. All listen and participate
2. Discussion of planets

1. Understanding of key words
2. Correct orbits and order

Level 1 Activity
Students will choose a favorite planet from the book/video. They will write and illustrate a flip book about one planet, with pictures on the outside and facts on the inside.

Assessment
1. 3 facts
2. Neatness of work
3. Organization

Level 2 Activity
Students will work in pairs to compare/contrast two planets using a Venn diagram.

Assessment
1. Accuracy of information
2. Organization
3. Clearly shows similarities and differences

Level 3 Activity
Students will write a short reader's theater presentation highlighting 2 facts about each planet and present it to the class.

Assessment
1. Factual information
2. Includes all planets
3. Interesting to class
4. Group cooperation

Whole Class Culminating Activity
1. The flip books and Venn diagrams will be shared with the class.
2. All students will listen to the reader's theater presentations.

Assessment
1. Discussion of major information learned
2. Good listening skills
3. Questions about planets to readers

Orbit Around the Sun Simulation

Objectives

Students will learn that:

1. The planets orbit around the sun for different lengths of time depending on the location of the planet.
2. When the planet goes around the sun one full time that is the end of the planet's year.
3. A year on one planet is a different amount of time compared to a year on another planet.
4. The planet's location in relation to the sun determines the planet's temperature.

Directions Divide students into groups of ten. Each student becomes the sun or one of the planets. Props each will carry are noted in parentheses. Planets are listed in their order from the sun.

1. Sun	Light and energy source for the planets (Light bulb)
2. Mercury	Covered by craters and very hot (Paper fan)
3. Venus	Hot and covered by thick clouds (Cotton cloud)
4. Earth	Teaming with all sorts of life (Green plant)
5. Mars	Named the red planet because of a large volcano (Red circle)
6. Jupiter	The biggest planet (Beach ball)
7. Saturn	Has beautiful rings made of ice (Hula hoop)
8. Uranus	Has many rings (Slinky tied around waist)
9. Neptune	Very cold and blue (Gloves, scarf, cap, blue circle)
10. Pluto	Smallest planet - or large ice ball - (Gloves, scarf, cap, golf ball)

Find a large area such as the school gym or playground. Mark off nine orbits around a central area. Place each child from the group of 10 in his or her correct place. The sun will stand still while the other nine children orbit around. Each child must be sure not to orbit ahead of the planet on their left (the one closer to the sun than they are). When a planet completes his orbit, he will stay in position until all the planets have made one orbit.

Repeat the activity so that each child in the class gets to participate.

Discussion

Discuss the following concepts and ideas with your students at the end of this activity.

*   *A year on a planet is the time it takes to orbit the sun. Some planets have longer years than others.*

*   *The closer the planet is to the sun, the hotter its temperature is.*

*   *Planets have specific identifying characteristics.*

*   *Planets also spin on their axis, creating day and night. How could we demonstrate this?*

Reproducible

TIERED ASSIGNMENT LESSON/UNIT PLANNING FORM

Unit/Subject/Theme: _____

Objectives:

Whole Class Activities   **Assessment**

Level 1 Activities   **Assessment**

Level 2 Activities   **Assessment**

Level 3 Activities   **Assessment**

Whole Class Culminating Activity   **Assessment**

Bibliography

Ashcraft, Michael. "The Day We Unplugged the TV." Orlando Sentinel Florida Magazine 29 September 1996.

Balsamo, Kathy L. Thematic Activities for Student Portfolios. Dayton OH: Pieces of Learning, 1994.

Clark, Barbara. Growing Up Gifted. New York: Macmillan Publishing Company, 1992.

Coil, Carolyn. Becoming an Achiever: A Student Guide. Dayton OH: Pieces of Learning, 1994.

Coil, Carolyn. Motivating Underachievers: 172 Strategies for Success. Dayton OH: Pieces of Learning, 1992.

Coil, Carolyn. Teaching Tools for the 21st Century. Dayton OH: Pieces of Learning, 1997.

Coutts, Cherylann. "Ready, set, summer!" Woman's Day 13 May 1997.

Cummings, Carol and Kevin P. Haggerty. "Raising Healthy Children." Educational Leadership May 1997.

Elias, Marilyn. "Praising Effort not Brains." USA Today 11 June 1997.

Frymier, Jack. Growing Up Is Risky Business and Schools Are Not to Blame. Bloomington IN: Phi Delta Kappa 1992.

Given, Barbara K. "Food for Thought." Educational Leadership November 1998.

Goleman, Daniel. Emotional Intelligence. New York: Bantam Books, 1995.

Hatcher, Ruth R. and Beth N. Pond. "Standardizing Organizational Skills for Student Success." Phi Delta Kappan May 1998.

"High School Students and Work." National Public Radio, 9 November 1998.

Jensen, Eric. "Teaching with the Brain in Mind." Alexandria VA: Association for Supervision and Curriculum Development, 1998.

Johnson, Nancy L. Active Questioning. Dayton OH: Pieces of Learning, 1995.

Johnson, Nancy L. Questioning Makes the Difference. Dayton OH: Pieces of Learning, 1990.

Johnson, Nancy L. Thinking is the Key. Dayton OH: Pieces of Learning, 1992.

Kersey, Katherine. Helping Your Child Handle Stress. Washington, D.C.: Acropolis Books Ltd., 1986.

Loupe, Diane. "Only Those Who Try Risk Failing." Atlanta Journal Constitution 10 May 1998.

Marklein, Mary Beth. "Are Kids Tested to Death?" USA Today 7 October 1997.

McClellan, Mary. "Why Blame the Schools?" Research Bulletin No. 12, Phi Delta Kappa March 1994.

Miles, Karen. "Help Your Child Excel." Readers Digest September 1995.

Palar, Barbara Hall. "Schools out!" Better Homes and Gardens June 1995.

Ratnesar, Romesh. "The Homework Ate My Family." Time Magazine 25 January 1999.

"Reaping the Benefits." AAHE Bulletin. April 1998.

Selye, Hans. The Stress of Life. New York: McGraw-Hill Book Company, 1978.

Sisk, Dorothy. Creative Teaching of the Gifted. New York: McGraw-Hill Book Company, 1987.

Sisk, Dorothy. "Encounter lessons: Tapping the Fantasy of the Gifted." Gifted Child Quarterly 1979.

Steele, Kathleen. Involving Parents in Schools. Dayton OH: Pieces of Learning, 1996.

Tomlinson, Carol Ann. How to Differentiate Instruction in Mixed-Ability Classrooms. Alexandria VA: Association for Supervision and Curriculum Development, 1995.

Viadero, Debra. "Students Reading Skills Fall Short." Education Week 22 September 1993.

Encouraging Achievement

**Traits and
Characteristics**

**The Brain
and Learning**

**The Role
of the School**

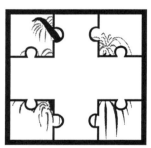

**Work, Challenges,
Learning from Failure,
Responsibility**

**The Role
of the Family**

**Dealing With
Children's Stress**

**Problems of Society
and Pop Culture**

**Independent
Learning Activities**

**Creative
Lesson Planning**